The
Ultimate Little
COCKTAIL
BOOK

RAY FOLEY

Copyright © 1998, 2006, 2011 by Ray Foley
Cover and internal design © 2011 by Sourcebooks, Inc.
Cover design by Krista Joy Johnson/Sourcebooks
Cover and internal illustration by Krista Joy Johnson/Sourcebooks

Sourcebooks and the colophon are registered trademarks of Sourcebooks, Inc.

Published by Sourcebooks, Inc.
P.O. Box 4410, Naperville, Illinois 60567-4410
(630) 961-3900
Fax: (630) 961-2168
www.sourcebooks.com

Originally published in 1998.

The Library of Congress has catalogued the first edition as follows:

Foley, Ray.
  The ultimate little cocktail book / Ray Foley.
    p. cm.
  Includes index.
  1. Alcoholic beverages. 2. Cocktails. I. Title.
  TX951.F59464 2006
  641.8'74—dc22

                    2005037947

          Printed and bound in Canada.
          WC 10 9 8 7 6 5 4 3 2 1

Dedicated to Emma.

CONTENTS

ACKNOWLEDGMENTS

To the amazing staff at Sourcebooks, especially Kelly Bale.

Peter Lynch for his foresight and having great taste in his selection of books.

Dominique Raccah for being Dominique Raccah.

Lauren Saccone for being a great person.

Jaclyn Marie Foley, the number one person in my life.

All the readers of *Bartender Magazine* and www.bartender.com and all the bartenders in the USA!

Special thanks: Jimmy Zazzali, Matt Wojciak, John Cowan, Michael Cammarano, Marvin Solomon, Millie Rinaldi, Laura Keegan, Meredith and Lindsay Scharf, Linda Saccone, Dave Conroy, Eugene Desimone, Robert Suffredini, Rene Bardel, Hymie Lipschitz, Joe Bonanno, Howard and De Wilson, and William and Amy Foley—the other tribe.

And for supplying all the ingredients in this

mixture and their tremendous support and help: Greg Cohen at Patron Tequila, Chester Brandes, Timo Sutinen, Carolina Marino and Michael Brandes from Sobieski Vodka and Imperial Brands, Vic Morrison at McCormick Distilling, Michel Roux and Jim Nikola at Crillon Importers, the great folks at Bacardi, Jose Cuervo, Diageo, Tabasco, The Food Group, SKYY Spirits, Cointreau, Joel Fishman from Tree Ripe, William Grant and Sons, Norton Cooper at Charles Jacquin et Cie, Bill Anderson at Infinium Spirits, the gracious assistance from Brown-Forman, Max Shapira, Parker Beam, and Edward DiMuro from Heaven Hill Distilleries, Jose Suarez and Jake Jacobsen at Coco Lopez, the wonderful cooperation from Pernod Ricard, David Rotunno from Mizkan Americas, and all our friends from Angostura Bitters.

And a special tip to Ryan Peter Foley (the best).

INTRODUCTION

As a bartender for more than thirty years and publisher of *Bartender* magazine for thirty-two years, I now have the honor of presenting *The Ultimate Little Cocktail Book.*

I started collecting cocktail recipe books more than thirty years ago, and my collection now consists of more than 1,750 different books from 1862 to the present day. Many new products and cocktails have been created since 1862. With the influx of new products, many new cocktails have become as popular as the old standards. We have included in this guide the old standards as well as the more popular cocktails of the 90s and into the millennium.

I have also selected the finest ingredients to be represented in *The Ultimate Little Cocktail Book.* After all, when preparing a great steak, you must start with a great piece of meat. Likewise, by using the best liquor, you create the ultimate cocktail. The proof is in the taste. Use premium brands at all times. They represent your cocktail, your establishment, and you.

. . .

We have not included drink recipes with items you'll have difficulty finding (i.e., Italian blue olives, Chinese sesame syrup, New Zealand kumquat mix, etc.).

Drinks are listed alphabetically by liquor in the table of contents.

Enjoy *The Ultimate Little Cocktail Book*. But, please, remember not to drink in excess. Moderation is the key word. Good judgment for yourself and your guests is most important to any successful party. Drinking and driving do not mix! The cocktail recipes herein are for your pleasure. Enjoy in moderation.

CHEERS,

Raymond P. Foley

. . .

Publisher's Note: This book and the recipes contained herein are intended for those of a legal drinking age. Please drink responsibly and ensure you and your guests have a designated driver when consuming alcoholic beverages.

Raw Egg Warning: Some recipes contained in this book call for the use of raw eggs. The Food and Drug Administration advises caution in consuming raw and lightly cooked eggs, due to the slight risk of salmonella or other food-borne illness. To reduce this risk, the FDA recommends that you use only fresh, clean, properly refrigerated and pasteurized eggs with intact shells. Always wash hands, cooking utensils, equipment, and work surfaces with warm, soapy water before and after they come in contact with eggs.

Aperol Betty

2 parts Aperol liqueur
1 part grapefruit juice
1 part orange juice
Ice cubes

Shake and blend.

Aperol Spritz

3 parts Prosecco
2 parts Aperol liqueur
Splash soda or seltzer
Ice cubes
½ slice orange for garnish

Garnish with the orange slice.

Asti Martini

4 oz. well-chilled Martini & Rossi Asti
½ oz. extra dry vermouth
Dash Chambord
Fresh raspberry for garnish

Add well-chilled Asti to the remaining ingredients and serve in a champagne flute. Garnish with a fresh raspberry.

B&B Manhattan

2 parts Benedictine
1 part Martini & Rossi sweet vermouth
Dash Angostura bitters
Maraschino cherry for garnish

Shake and garnish with the cherry.

Baracas Cocktail

2 oz. Punt e Mes vermouth
1 oz. Fernet-Branca
Ice cubes

Pour all ingredients into a shaker with ice. Strain into a cocktail glass.

Bitch Slap

Fernet-Branca Menta
Beer for chaser

Pour into a shot glass and drink beer as a chaser (Hymie Special).

Casino Royale Cocktail, Shaken Not Stirred

3 parts gin
1 part vodka
½ part Lillet white vermouth
5 ice cubes
Lemon twist for garnish

Classic Pernod

1 part Pernod
5 parts water
Ice cubes

Pour 1 part Pernod in a glass. Add 5 parts water. Add ice to fill glass.

Corpse Reviver

Ice cubes
1 ½ oz. brandy
1 oz. white crème de menthe
½ oz. Fernet-Branca

In a mixing glass half-filled with ice cubes, combine remaining ingredients. Stir well. Strain into a cocktail glass.

Dubonnet Cocktail

1 oz. dry gin
1 oz. Dubonnet Rouge
Dash orange bitters
Ice cubes
Lemon twist for garnish

Combine in ice shaker. Shake. Strain into martini glass and garnish with twist of lemon.

Fedora

¼ oz. Fernet-Branca
Ice cubes
2 ½ oz. Templeton Rye whiskey
½ oz. Punt e Mes vermouth
Lemon or orange twist for garnish

Pour the Fernet-Branca into an ice-filled shaker and "wash the ice" by stirring the liquid, then drain. Combine the rye and vermouth into the shaker. Stir vigorously and serve up in a martini or sherbet glass. Garnish with a twist of lemon or orange.

FERinterNET.com

1 ½ oz. Fernet-Branca Menta

Serve on the rocks by your computer.

Fernandito

2 oz. Fernet-Branca
3 oz. frozen cola
Lime slice for garnish
3 ice cubes

Pour Fernet-Branca into a tall tumbler. Fill with frozen cola. Add a lime slice and 3 ice cubes.

Fernet Coffee

1 American coffee with sugar
1 ½ oz. Fernet-Branca
2 tsp. whipped cream

Pour the Fernet-Branca and the coffee in a glass and add the cream on top.

Fernet Negroni

1 oz. Baffert's Gin
1 oz. Fernet-Branca
¾ oz. Punt e Mes vermouth
Ice cubes
Orange twist for garnish

Combine first three ingredients over ice in a shaker. Stir until chilled and serve up in a cocktail glass. Garnish with orange twist.

French Fizz

5 parts champagne
1 part Pernod
Ice cubes

Pour champagne and Pernod into a tall glass filled with ice. Mix well.

Frozen Lillet Red

2 parts Lillet Red vermouth
1 part Hendrick's gin
1 part peach liqueur
Ice cubes
1 wedge peach for garnish

Hanky Panky Cocktail

1 ½ oz. Baffert's gin
1 ½ oz. Punt e Mes vermouth
2 dashes Fernet-Branca
1 orange peel for garnish

Shake well and strain into cocktail glass. Squeeze orange peel on top. (Listed in *The Savoy Cocktail Book*.)

Hot Houdini

2 oz. Fernet-Branca
3 drops Tabasco

Put ingredients in shot glass. Make the drink disappear fast.

Italian Bull

2 oz. Fernet-Branca
1.84 oz. can Red Bull

Add Fernet to Red Bull and chug.

Limo Rider

1 oz. Fernet-Branca
½ oz. Borghettie sambuca
½ oz. Seagram's vodka

Serve over ice or in a shot glass.

Martini & Rossi "007" Cocktail

2 parts Martini & Rossi extra dry vermouth
2 parts orange juice
Splash grenadine
Ice cubes

Stir. Serve on the rocks.

Martini & Rossi Cooler

2 oz. Martini & Rossi extra dry vermouth
Dash grenadine
Club soda to fill
Ice cubes
Orange slice for garnish

Pour first three ingredients into large glass filled with ice. Garnish with an orange slice.

Martini & Rossi Sunset

3 oz. orange juice
1 ½ oz. Martini & Rossi extra dry vermouth
½ oz. triple sec
Splash grenadine
Ice cubes
Orange slice for garnish

Pour first four ingredients into a shaker filled with ice. Hand-stir and strain into a rocks glass or tall glass over ice. Garnish with an orange slice.

Martini Sweet

⅔ oz. dry gin
⅓ oz. Martini & Rossi Rosso vermouth
4–5 ice cubes

Prepare in a mixing glass. Serve in a cocktail glass.

Menta B

1 oz. brandy
½ oz. Fernet-Branca Menta

Pour over ice or serve as a shot.

Negroni

½ oz. Campari
½ oz. dry gin
½ oz. Martini & Rossi extra dry vermouth
Ice cubes

Serve in rocks glass over ice.

Perfect Manhattan

1 ½ oz. bourbon
¼ oz. Martini & Rossi extra dry vermouth
¼ oz. Martini & Rossi Rosso vermouth
1-2 dashes bitters

Stir. Serve straight up or on the rocks.

Pernod French Kiss

4 parts orange juice
1 part Pernod
Ice cubes
Dash grenadine

Mix orange juice and Pernod in a cocktail shaker with ice. Strain into a martini glass. Add grenadine and allow it to settle at the bottom.

The Princess

1 part Martini & Rossi Rosso vermouth
1 part rum
Ice cubes

Stir over ice.

Queen Bee

1 oz. Baffert's gin
1 oz. Fernet-Branca

Pour over ice or serve as a shot.

Red Roman

2 oz. Fernet-Branca
1 oz. Seagram's vodka
Dash grenadine
Ice cubes

Stir. Serve on the rocks.

Ricard Pastis

1 part Ricard
5 parts cold water
Ice cubes to fill

Pour Ricard in a glass. Add water and ice to fill.

Riverside

½ oz. dry gin
½ oz. Martini & Rossi extra dry vermouth
½ oz. Martini & Rossi Rosso vermouth
½ oz. orange juice
Ice cubes

Shake. Serve over ice.

Rosso Sunset

3 oz. orange juice
1 ½ oz. Martini & Rossi Rosso vermouth
½ oz. triple sec
Splash grenadine
Ice cubes

Shake. Serve over ice.

Russian Branca

1 oz. Fernet-Branca
1 oz. Seagram's vodka

Serve over ice or in a shot glass.

Silk Hankie

1 oz. Borgetti sambuca
1 oz. Fernet-Branca Menta

Serve on the rocks or as a shot.

Sparkling Fernet

2 oz. Fernet-Branca
Ice cubes
1 slice lemon or lime
Tonic water to fill

Pour Fernet over ice cubes in a long drink glass.
Add a slice of lemon or lime and fill with tonic
water.

Stomach Reviver

1 oz. brandy
1 oz. Fernet-Branca
3 dashes Angostura bitters
Ice cubes

Pour first three ingredients into a shaker with
ice. Shake. Strain into a shot glass. Knock it back.
Breathe a sigh of relief.

Suze Gimlet

1 ½ oz. Suze
½ oz. lemon juice
½ oz. lime juice

Combine ingredients. Shake in an iced strainer,
and strain into a chilled cocktail glass.

Sweet Red Kiss

1 ½ oz. Dubonnet Rouge
⅓ oz. Absolut Kurant vodka
⅓ oz. Chambord
Splash cranberry juice
Splash orange juice
Splash pineapple juice
Orange slice or twist for garnish

Serve up with a sugar rim. Garnish with orange slice or twist.

Tequila Menta

1 oz. Casa Noble tequila
½ oz. Fernet-Branca Menta

Pour over ice or serve as a shot.

Three Guys from Italy

1 oz. amaretto
1 oz. Borghetti sambuca
1 oz. Fernet-Branca Menta

Serve as a shot.

The Tonic Twist

4 oz. tonic
2 oz. Martini & Rossi extra dry vermouth
Lime twist for garnish

Add a twist of lime.

Vermouth Cassis

2 oz. Martini & Rossi extra dry vermouth
½ oz. crème de cassis
Ice cubes
Club soda to fill
Lemon twist or wedge for garnish

Combine the first two ingredients in a tall glass over ice, fill with club soda, and garnish with the lemon twist or wedge.

Vermouth Cocktail

2 oz. Martini & Rossi Rosso vermouth
Dash bitters
Dash cherry juice
Ice cubes

Stir well. Serve on the rocks.

Vermouth Cooler

2 oz. Martini & Rossi extra dry vermouth
Dash grenadine
Ice cubes
Club soda to fill

Serve in large glass with ice. Fill with club soda.

Western Rose

1 ¼ oz. dry gin
¼ oz. brandy
¼ oz. Martini & Rossi extra dry vermouth
Ice cubes

Shake. Serve in rocks glass with ice.

Winter

2 oz. tonic water
1 ½ oz. Aperol liqueur
1 oz. Fernet-Branca
Ice cubes
Orange slice for garnish

Pour first three ingredients in a tall tumbler and
mix them. Add some ice cubes and serve with an
orange slice.

Yodel

Ice cubes
1 ½ oz. Fernet-Branca
1 ½ oz. orange juice
Club soda to fill

Fill rocks glass with ice. Add Fernet and orange
juice. Stir. Fill with club soda.

BITTERS

Affinity Cocktail

1 oz. blended Scotch whisky
½ oz. dry vermouth
½ oz. sweet vermouth
2 drops Angostura bitters
1 tsp. sugar
Lemon twist for garnish
Maraschino cherry for garnish

Place first five ingredients in an ice-filled shaker and shake vigorously. Strain into a chilled cocktail glass. Garnish with the lemon twist and maraschino cherry.

Bahama Mama

2 oz. sweetened pineapple juice
1 oz. coconut liqueur
1 oz. gold rum
1 oz. unsweetened orange juice
1 oz. white rum
½ oz. grenadine syrup
3 dashes Angostura bitters
Ice cubes
2 maraschino cherries for garnish
Orange slice for garnish
Pineapple wedge for garnish

Place first seven ingredients in a shaker and shake vigorously. Strain into an ice-filled Collins or Poco Grande glass. Garnish with maraschino cherries, orange slice, and pineapple wedge.

Boss's Daughter

1 ½ oz. gold rum
½ oz. amaretto
2 dashes Angostura aromatic bitters
2 dashes Angostura orange bitters
Splash lemonade
Orange slice for garnish

Build in a rocks glass and stir. Garnish with an orange slice.

Breakfast in Trinidad

2 oz. Angostura 1919 rum
½ oz. lemon juice
¼ oz. Angostura orange bitters
¼ oz. apricot brandy
2 tsp. apricot jam
Ice cubes
Orange slice for garnish

Add all ingredients to Boston shaker and stir. Shake vigorously with ice. Strain over cubed ice into a rocks glass. Garnish with an orange slice.

Bronx Cocktail

1 ½ oz. gin
1 ¼ oz. fresh orange juice
¼ oz. dry vermouth
¼ oz. sweet vermouth
Dash Angostura orange bitters
Orange twist for garnish

Place first five ingredients in an ice-filled shaker and shake vigorously. Strain into a chilled cocktail glass. Garnish with the orange twist.

Dark 'n' Handsome

1 ½ oz. gold rum
¼ oz. lime juice
5 dashes Angostura aromatic bitters
Ginger beer to top
Lime wedge for garnish

Build in a highball glass. Garnish with a lime wedge.

Did It My Way

1 ½ oz. dark rum
Lime squeeze
2 dashes Angostura aromatic bitters
Grapefruit juice to top
Lime wedge for garnish

Build in a highball glass. Garnish with a lime wedge.

Fruit Daiquiri (Blended)

2 oz. white rum
1 ½ oz. fruit purée or nectar, as desired
½ oz. fresh lime juice
½ oz. triple sec
2 dashes Angostura aromatic bitters
1 ½ scoops ice cubes
Lime wheel for garnish
4 fruit wedges, as desired

Blend all ingredients with the ice until firm and smooth. Pour into a goblet. Garnish with lime wheel and fruit wedges.

Kaboom

2 oz. dark rum
½ oz. pear purée
3 dashes Angostura bitters
1 tsp. brown sugar
White chocolate curls for garnish

Stir in a rocks glass. Garnish with white chocolate.

Last Call

1 oz. Angostura 1824 Rum
½ oz. vanilla liqueur
¼ oz. chocolate syrup
¼ oz. Crème de Myrtille de Montagne liqueur
¼ oz. pineapple juice
2 dashes Angostura bitters
1 egg white
Ice cubes
Freshly ground nutmeg for garnish

Dry shake and add ice. Shake and strain into a
martini glass. Garnish with ground nutmeg.

Manhattan

2 ½ oz. rye whiskey
1 oz. sweet vermouth
2 dashes Angostura bitters
Ice cubes
Maraschino cherry for garnish

Stir first three ingredients for 1 minute with ice in mixing glass and strain into chilled cocktail glass. Garnish with maraschino cherry.

The Margadale Dram

2 oz. Bunnahabhain 12-Year-Old Scotch
½ oz. sweet vermouth
¼ oz. fresh yellow capsicum, shredded
⅛ oz. fresh rosemary
Dash Angostura bitters
Drunken fresh oyster for garnish

Stir firmly and strain into a chilled martini glass. Garnish with drunken fresh oyster.

 ANDY GRIFFITHS, AUSTRALIA
FINALIST IN ANGOSTURA GLOBAL COCKTAIL
CHALLENGE 2011

Martini (Traditional)

1 ½ oz. gin
¾ oz. dry vermouth
1–2 dashes Angostura bitters
Olive and/or lemon twist for garnish

Stir for 1 minute with ice in mixing glass, and strain into chilled martini glass. Garnish with an olive and/or lemon twist.

Pedro/Juan Collins

1 ½ oz. silver tequila
1 ¼ oz. simple syrup
1 oz. fresh lemon juice
2 dashes Angostura orange bitters
Ice cubes
Club soda to top
Lemon wedge for garnish
Maraschino cherry for garnish
Orange slice for garnish

Shake first four ingredients in an ice-filled shaker and strain into a Collins glass filled with ice. Top with club soda and stir gently. Garnish with the lemon wedge, maraschino cherry, and orange slice.

Perfect Manhattan

1 ½ oz. rye whiskey
1 ½ oz. sweet vermouth
2 dashes Angostura aromatic bitters
Ice cubes
Maraschino cherry for garnish

Stir first three ingredients for 1 minute with ice in mixing glass and strain into chilled cocktail glass. Garnish with a maraschino cherry.

Pink Gin

2 ½ oz. gin
3 dashes Angostura aromatic bitters
Dash Angostura orange bitters
Ice cubes
Splash tonic water to taste (optional)

Shake first three ingredients in an ice-filled shaker and strain into ice-filled old-fashioned glass. Stir. A splash of tonic water may be added to taste.

Rob Roy

2 ½ oz. blended Scotch whisky
1 oz. sweet vermouth
2 dashes Angostura aromatic bitters
Ice cubes
Lemon twist for garnish

Stir first three ingredients for 1 minute with ice in mixing glass and strain into chilled cocktail glass. Garnish with lemon twist.

Rum 'n' Bass

1 ½ oz. Angostura 1919 rum
¾ oz. lemon juice
½ oz. triple sec
¼ oz. vanilla syrup
2 dashes Angostura aromatic bitters
Ice cubes
1 12-oz. can ginger beer to top
2 orange wheels for garnish

Add first five ingredients and shake. Strain into a Collins glass over ice and top with ginger beer. Garnish with 2 orange wheels sunk in glass.

Rum Sour

2 oz. gold rum
1 oz. simple syrup
¾ oz. fresh lime or lemon juice
Dash Angostura orange bitters
Ice cubes
Lime or orange twist for garnish

Shake ingredients with ice and strain into sour glass. Garnish with a lime or orange twist.

Smokey Nutini

2 oz. Bunnahabhain Single Malt Scotch
¼ oz. Monin Toffee Nut Syrup
¼ oz. fresh lime juice
5 dashes Angostura aromatic bitters
Almonds for garnish

In a mixing glass with ice, add all ingredients and stir well. Strain into a chilled martini glass. Drop on a few almonds and serve.

 YANGDUP LAMA, INDIA
FINALIST IN ANGOSTURA GLOBAL COCKTAIL
CHALLENGE 2011

Sweet Martini

1 ½ oz. gin
1 ½ oz. sweet vermouth
Dash Angostura aromatic bitters
Orange twist for garnish

Shake all ingredients and strain into chilled martini glass. Garnish with an orange twist.

Tequila Old-Fashioned

½ oz. water
1 ½ tsp. sugar
2 seedless orange slices
3 maraschino cherries
2 dashes Angostura aromatic bitters
2 oz. gold tequila
Ice cubes

Muddle first five ingredients in the bottom of an old-fashioned glass. Add gold tequila and stir thoroughly. Add ice cubes and stir again thoroughly.

Tobagonian Doctor

1 ½ oz. Angostura 1919 rum
¾ oz. apricot brandy
¼ oz. Angostura orange bitters
Ice cubes
Lemon twist for garnish

Put first three ingredients in a mixing glass and
stir over ice. Strain into coupe glass and garnish
with lemon twist.

BRANDY, COGNAC, AND PISCO

Beach Cruiser

4 oz. orange juice
3 oz. cranberry juice
1 ½ oz. Korbel XS Extra Smooth brandy
Ice cubes
Lime wedge for garnish

Combine juices and Korbel KS brandy. Shake well and serve over ice. Garnish with the lime wedge.

Between the Sheets

1 oz. Korbel California VSOP Gold Reserve
   brandy
1 oz. Malibu Original Caribbean rum
1 oz. triple sec
1 tsp. lemon juice
Ice cubes
Orange twist for garnish

Combine first four ingredients with ice. Shake
and pour into cocktail glass. Garnish with orange
twist.

Brandy Alexander

3 oz. Korbel California VSOP Gold Reserve
   brandy
2 oz. cream
1 oz. dark crème de cacao
Pinch grated nutmeg

Shake ingredients and pour into a chilled cocktail glass. Sprinkle with nutmeg.

Brandy Old-Fashioned

½ oz. water
3 maraschino cherries
2 seedless orange slices
2 dashes Angostura aromatic bitters
1 ½ tsp. granulated sugar
2 oz. brandy or cognac
Ice cubes

Muddle first five ingredients in the bottom of an old-fashioned glass. Add brandy/cognac and stir thoroughly. Add cubed ice to muddled ingredients in old-fashioned glass and stir thoroughly.

Brandy Sunset

1 ½ oz. Korbel California VSOP Gold Reserve
    brandy
2 oz. 7-Up
1 oz. orange juice to fill
⅛ oz. grenadine to float
Maraschino cherry for garnish

Pour ingredients over ice into tall glass. Garnish with cherry.

CB Coffee Royal

1 tsp. superfine sugar
2 tbsp. hot coffee, plus extra to fill
1 ½ oz. Christian Brothers brandy
Whipped cream

In a coffee mug, dissolve sugar in coffee. Add brandy and fill with hot coffee. Top with a dollop of whipped cream.

CB Honey Fizz

2 oz. Christian Brothers Honey brandy
1 oz. club soda
Squeeze fresh lime juice
Ice cubes
Lime twist for garnish

Pour first three ingredients over ice and stir. Garnish with a lime twist.

Cello Martini

1 oz. Cointreau
1 oz. Korbel California VSOP Gold Reserve
  brandy
½ oz. limoncello
Juice ½ lemon
Ice cubes
Coarse sugar for rim
Lemon twist for garnish

Shake first four ingredients with ice. Strain into martini glass with sugar rim. Garnish with lemon twist.

Dirty Momma

1 oz. coffee liqueur
1 oz. cream
1 oz. Korbel California VSOP Gold Reserve brandy
Ice cubes

Pour first three ingredients over ice and stir.

Dutch Treat

3 oz. hot chocolate
1 ¼ oz. Asbach Uralt brandy
Dollop whipped cream

Serve in mug and top with whipped cream. Add straw.

Floating Orchid

3 oz. pineapple juice
1 oz. Korbel California VSOP Gold Reserve
    brandy
½ oz. triple sec
Korbel extra dry champagne to top
Lemon twist for garnish

Combine the pineapple juice, brandy, and triple sec with ice. Shake and pour into cocktail glass. Top with champagne. Garnish with lemon twist.

French 75

1 ½ oz. Korbel California VSOP Gold Reserve
    brandy
1 oz. fresh lemon juice
1 oz. simple syrup
Korbel extra dry champagne for float

Shake the brandy, fresh lemon juice, and simple syrup with ice. Strain and pour into champagne flute. Float with champagne.

Honey Bear

1 oz. Christian Brothers Honey brandy

Serve in a shot glass.

Keoke Coffee

1 oz. Korbel California VSOP Gold Reserve
     brandy
½ oz. coffee liqueur
½ oz. dark crème de cacao
Freshly brewed coffee to fill
Dollop whipped cream
Chocolate shavings for garnish

In a coffee mug, mix brandy, coffee liqueur, and crème de cacao. Fill with fresh-brewed coffee. Top with whipped cream and chocolate shavings.

The Lei Maker

2 oz. pineapple juice
1 ½ oz. Korbel California VSOP Gold Reserve
     brandy
1 oz. Domaine de Canton ginger liqueur
Ice cubes
1 oz. Sprite
Orchid for garnish

Shake the first three ingredients with ice. Pour into tall cocktail glass on the rocks. Float with Sprite. Garnish with the orchid.

Old-Fashioned

Maraschino cherry
Orange slice
1 tsp. sugar
2 dashes Angostura bitters
1 ½ oz. Korbel California VSOP Gold Reserve
    brandy
Ice cubes
Splash 7-Up to top

Muddle maraschino cherry and orange slice with sugar and bitters. Add the brandy and ice cubes. Stir, and top with 7-Up.

Peach Cobbler

¾ fresh peach, pitted and sliced, plus 1 slice
    for garnish
½ oz. simple syrup
Ice cubes
1 ½ oz. Korbel XS brandy
Splash soda water to top

Place peach slices in mixing glass with simple syrup. Muddle. Fill with ice. Add Korbel XS brandy. Shake and pour into glass. Top with soda water. Garnish with the remaining peach slice.

Pink Elephant

1 ½ oz. Korbel XS brandy
1 oz. Malibu Original Caribbean rum
½ oz. each cranberry juice and pineapple juice

Pour brandy and rum in rocks glass. Top with juices.

Pure Honey

2 oz. Christian Brothers Honey brandy

Pour over ice and enjoy.

Ruedesheimer Coffee

3 sugar cubes
1-2 parts Asbach Uralt brandy
Hot coffee to fill
Whipped cream with vanilla for garnish
Grated chocolate for garnish

Place sugar in a warmed coffee cup. Add the brandy, set aflame, stir, and allow to burn for a good minute. Fill up with good hot coffee to within an inch of the top of the cup. Stir well. Cover with a layer of whipped cream spiced with vanilla, and sprinkle with grated chocolate.

Sidecar

1 oz. fresh lemon juice
1 oz. Korbel California VSOP Gold Reserve
   brandy
1 oz. triple sec
Coarse sugar for rim
Lemon twist for garnish

Shake ingredients and pour into martini glass
with sugar rim. Garnish with lemon twist.

Skinny Dip

2 oz. Korbel XS brandy
1 oz. cranberry juice
1 oz. orange juice
1 oz. pineapple juice
Ice cubes
Splash Sprite
Orange wedge for garnish
Maraschino cherry for garnish

Shake brandy and juices with ice. Pour into cocktail glass. Top with Sprite. Garnish with orange
wedge and cherry.

Stinger

¾ oz. Asbach Uralt brandy
¾ oz. white crème de menthe

Shake well with ice. Strain into chilled cocktail glass.

Unpublished Hemingway

1 ½ oz. Asbach Uralt brandy
¼ oz. Grand Marnier

Mix in a brandy snifter.

The Wilshire

5 oz. cranberry juice
1 oz. Korbel XS brandy
Ice cubes
Lime slice for garnish

Combine in a tall glass over ice. Stir well. Garnish with lime slice.

Pisco Porton
Brandy Recipes

Pisco is a strong, colorless grape brandy produced in Peru and Chile. It was developed by Spanish settlers in the sixteenth century. Pisco takes its name from the conical pottery in which it was originally aged, which was also the name of one of the sites where it was produced: Pisco. In modern times, it continues to be produced in winemaking regions of Peru and Chile. The right to produce and promote pisco has been the matter of legal disputes between Chile and Peru.

Pisco Porton is an ultra-premium white spirit that is versatile in cocktails and offers complexity with a delicate finish when savored on its own. Born from grapes that grow in the shadows of the Andes Mountains, Pisco Porton is artisanally crafted at Hacienda La Caravedo distillery in Inca, Peru. Building on the heritage and traditions of this distillery, which was founded in 1684 and is the oldest in the Americas, Pisco Porton combines centuries-old methods with state-of-the-art and ecofriendly technology to create a *mosto verde* pisco of unmatched quality.

1684

6 medium-sized sweet red grapes
1 tsp. agave
Ice cubes
1 ½ oz. Pisco Porton
¾ oz. simple syrup
1 oz. fresh lime juice
½ oz. St. Germain

In a shaker, muddle the grapes with the agave. Add ice and the rest of the ingredients. Shake and pour into a rock glass. Serve with a teaspoon.

Capitan

1 ½ oz. Pisco Porton
1 ½ oz. vermouth
Ice cubes
1 dash Angostura bitters
Maraschino cherry for garnish

Pour Pisco Porton and vermouth into a glass with ice. Add dash of bitters. Stir ingredients together until cool. Strain into a martini glass with a maraschino cherry resting at the bottom. For a sweeter taste, add ½ oz. sweet vermouth. For a drier drink, add an additional ½ oz. Pisco Porton.

Frozen Pisco & Lime Raspadilla

Ice cubes
2 ½ oz. Pisco Porton
½ oz. fresh lime juice
½ oz. Rose's Lime Juice
Lime slice for rim, plus one for garnish
Coarse sugar for rim

Fill blender with ice and wet ingredients. Blend until frozen. Rub the rim of a margarita glass with a lime slice so that the sugar will stick, then rim the glass with sugar and add blended ingredients. Garnish with a lime slice.

Made in Peru

2 thin cucumber slices (circles), plus two for garnish
Mint leaves
¾ oz. simple syrup
2 oz. Pisco Porton
1 oz. fresh lime juice

In a shaker, muddle 2 slices of cucumber with a handful of mint and simple syrup. Add Pisco Porton and lime juice. Shake and strain on the rocks. Garnish with remaining cucumber.

The Orient

2 oz. Pisco Porton marinated with lychee
Ice cubes
½ oz. sake
Lychee for garnish

Pour Pisco Porton and sake into a shaker with ice. Shake well and strain the contents into a martini glass. Garnish with a lychee.

Pink Passion

2 oz. Pisco Porton
1 oz. pomegranate juice
1 oz. tangerine juice
Sugar to taste
Ice cubes
Pomegranate seeds for garnish

Combine ingredients in a shaker with ice. Shake well and strain into a martini glass. Garnish with pomegranate seeds.

Pisco Punch

1 4-lb. pineapple, peeled, cut into 1-inch pieces
1 750-ml bottle Pisco Porton
2 cups simple syrup (1 cup hot water and 1
    cup fine sugar), divided
1 ½ tsp. grated lime peel
1 ½ tsp. grated white grapefruit peel
⅔ cup fresh lemon juice
12 pineapple spears for garnish

Place pineapple slices in covered jar. Pour Pisco
Porton over. Cover and refrigerate for two days,
shaking occasionally. Divide simple syrup
between two bowls. Mix grated lime peel into
one bowl and grated grapefruit peel into other
bowl. Cover and refrigerate both syrups over-
night. Strain Pisco Porton into pitcher. Discard
pineapple. Strain both syrups into Pisco Porton.
Add lemon juice. Stir to blend. Fill six cocktail
glasses with ice, then add punch. Garnish with
pineapple spears.

Makes 6 servings.

The History of Pisco in the United States: Pisco Punch

In the second half of the nineteenth century,
pisco was king in San Francisco's watering holes.
Back then, it was easier to ship pisco up the coast
from Peru than to transport whiskey overland
from the East Coast. Newly rich gold prospec-
tors, thirsty sailors, and eventually all of San

Francisco developed a robust appetite for pisco that lasted until the supply was cut off by prohibition in 1920. Pisco Punch was the most famous cocktail in San Francisco, made at the Bank Exchange on Montgomery and Washington by famous bar owner Duncan Nicol. At twenty-five cents, the drink was preposterously expensive yet incredibly popular. A true gentleman barkeeper, Nicol had a house rule that two pisco punches were enough for any patron of his bar. If a customer wanted a third, he had to walk around the long block and come back in to qualify as a new customer.

Pisco Sour

1 ½ oz. Pisco Porton
½ oz. fresh lime juice
½ oz. simple syrup
¼ oz. egg white
Ice cubes
1 dash Angostura bitters

Combine first four ingredients in a shaker with ice. Shake and strain contents into a chilled glass. Add a dash of bitters.

Porton Tini

1 ½ oz. Pisco Porton
1 oz. fresh lemon juice
1 oz. simple syrup
½ oz. vanilla liqueur
Ice cubes
1 oz. club soda
Lemon twist for garnish

Mix the first four ingredients in a shaker with ice. Strain into a martini glass. Top with club soda. Garnish with a lemon twist.

Saint Pisco Porton

2 thin cucumber slices (circles), plus 2 for
   garnish
Mint leaves
¾ oz. simple syrup
2 oz. Pisco Porton
1 oz. St. Germain
¾ oz. fresh lime juice
¾ oz. soda water

In a shaker, muddle 2 slices of cucumber with a handful of mint and simple syrup. Add Pisco Porton, St. Germain, lime juice, and soda water. Shake and strain on the rocks. Garnish with remaining cucumber.

Strawberry Peruvian Margarita

2 oz. Pisco Porton
1 ½ oz. fresh crushed strawberries or premium
    strawberry mix
1 oz. simple syrup
½ oz. fresh lime juice
Ice cubes
Strawberry for garnish

Combine the first four ingredients in a shaker
with ice and shake. Strain contents into a chilled
margarita glass. Garnish with a strawberry.

Strawberry Porton Tini

3 fresh crushed strawberries, plus 1 for garnish
1 ¼ oz. Pisco Porton
1 ¼ oz. soda water
¾ oz. fresh lime juice
¾ oz. simple syrup
½ oz. Monin Chipotle Pineapple Syrup
Ice cubes
Lime wedge for garnish

Mix all ingredients in a shaker with ice. Strain
into a cocktail glass. Garnish with a fresh strawberry and a lime wedge.

Submission

1 ¾ oz. Pisco Porton
¾ oz. Lillet Blanc
½ oz. Benedictine
Orange twist for garnish

Stir and strain into a coupe glass. Garnish with an orange twist.

Summer Session

4 medium-sized basil leaves
3 watermelon cubes
2 parts Pisco Porton
¾ part fresh lime juice
¾ part simple syrup
Fresh ground black pepper

Muddle basil and watermelon. Add the rest of the ingredients. Shake hard and strain into a coupe glass.

Ultimate Peruvian Margarita

1 oz. Grand Marnier
1 oz. Pisco Porton
1 oz. simple syrup
½ oz. fresh lemon juice
½ oz. fresh lime juice
Ice cubes
Lime wedge for garnish
Orange wedge for garnish

Shake first five ingredients with ice. Strain into a margarita glass. Garnish with a lime and orange wedge.

Vianef

1 oz. Drambuie liqueur
1 oz. Pisco Porton
¼ oz. Campari
¼ oz. lime juice
Lime twist for garnish
Orange wedge for garnish

Combine and chill all ingredients. Serve in a martini glass with a lime twist and orange wedge.

CORDIALS

Alarm Clock

1 part Drambuie liqueur
½ part Bacardi Select rum
½ part Dewar's White Label Blended Scotch
    whisky
Ice cubes

Shake and strain into a rocks glass.

Alexander

2 oz. cognac
1 oz. Marie Brizard Cocoa liqueur
½ oz. heavy cream

Shake. Serve in cocktail glass.

Ambrosia

1 oz. Laird's Applejack
¼ oz. brandy
¼ oz. Cointreau
¼ oz. fresh lemon juice
Ice cubes
Champagne to fill

Shake first four ingredients over ice. Strain into champagne flute. Fill with champagne.

Apres Sobieski

2 oz. Sobieski vodka
½ oz. Marie Brizard white crème de menthe
    liqueur

Shake with ice. Serve as a shot.

Apry Amour

2 ½ oz. Sobieski vodka
½ oz. Marie Brizard Apry liqueur
Ice cubes
Rose petal for garnish

Shake first two ingredients with ice. Strain into a martini glass. Garnish with a rose petal.

Backdraft

½ part Drambuie liqueur
½ part triple sec

Combine and serve in a shot glass.

Bellini

1 ½ oz. Marie Brizard peach liqueur
5 oz. champagne

Pour the liqueur into a champagne flute. Add the champagne.

Bent Nail

½ part Canadian whiskey
½ part Drambuie liqueur
1 tsp. Kirschwasser

Combine all ingredients in a cocktail shaker and strain into a rocks glass filled with ice.

Blackberry Alexander

1 oz. blackberries
1 ¼ oz. half-and-half
1 ¼ oz. Remy Martin VSOP cognac
1 ¼ oz. white crème de cacao
¼ oz. Cointreau

Muddle blackberries. Combine all ingredients. Shake and strain into a martini glass.

Black Tartan

1 part Dewar's White Label Blended Scotch whisky
¼ part coffee liqueur
¼ part Drambuie liqueur
¼ part Irish whiskey

Shake. Serve over rocks.

Blue Meanie

2 oz. sour mix
1 ½ oz. Sobieski vodka
½ oz. Marie Brizard blue curaçao liqueur

Shake with ice and strain into shot glass.

Bonnie Prince

1 ½ part Bombay Sapphire gin
¼ part Drambuie liqueur
¼ part white wine
Orange peel for garnish

Combine all ingredients in a cocktail shaker and shake well. Strain into a chilled martini cocktail glass and garnish with the orange peel.

Champagne Blitz

¼ oz. Marie Brizard white crème de menthe liqueur
3 oz. champagne

Pour crème de menthe into a champagne flute and fill with champagne.

Champagne Cassis

2 oz. Marie Brizard Black Currant liqueur
Champagne to top

Serve in champagne flute.

Champagne Cobbler

1 oz. Cointreau
½ oz. fresh lemon juice
Piper-Heidsieck champagne

Pour first two ingredients into flute. Top with champagne.

Cointreau Bubbles

Slice fresh lime
2 oz. Cointreau
Sparkling water or tonic
Small lime slice for garnish

Muddle lime in glass. Add Cointreau and top with sparkling water or tonic. Garnish with small slices of lime.

Cointreaupolitan

1 ½ oz. Cointreau
1 oz. cranberry juice
¾ oz. fresh lemon juice
Ice cubes

Shake all ingredients and strain into a chilled martini glass.

Cointreautini

2 ½ oz. Cointreau
Juice ½ lime
Ice cubes and crushed ice

Mix in a shaker with ice cubes. Shake vigorously.
Strain over crushed ice in a martini glass.

Cosmopolitan

1 ½ oz. vodka
1 oz. Cointreau
1 oz. cranberry juice
¾ oz. fresh lime juice
Orange twist for garnish

Shake and strain into a chilled martini glass.
Garnish with an orange twist.

Drambuie and Coffee

Freshly brewed coffee lightly sweetened with the
delicious flavor of Drambuie. Serve in a warm
glass and top with fresh cream. Equally pleas-
ing when served with hot tea instead of coffee.
Satisfying and distinctly different.

Dundee

Ice cubes, divided
1 ½ part Bombay Sapphire gin
1 part Dewar's White Label Blended Scotch
    whisky
1 ½ part Drambuie liqueur
1 tsp. lemon juice
Maraschino cherry for garnish
Lemon twist for garnish

Fill mixing glass with ice; add Bombay, Dewar's,
Drambuie, and lemon juice. Shake, strain into a
rocks glass, and add ice. Garnish with a cherry
and lemon twist.

Funky Monkey

1 ¾ oz. Marie Brizard banana liqueur
¾ oz. Marie Brizard white crème de cacao
    liqueur
¾ oz. rum
½ fresh ripe banana, peeled, for garnish

Blend. Garnish with banana.

Grasshopper

2 oz. Sobieski vodka
1 oz. cream or milk
½ oz. Marie Brizard green crème de menthe
    liqueur
½ oz. Marie Brizard white crème de cacao
    liqueur
Ice cubes

Shake and strain.

Kamikaze

1 ½ oz. vodka
¾ oz. Cointreau
¼ oz. fresh lemon juice

Shake and strain into a chilled martini glass.

Kilt Lifter

1 part Dewar's White Label Blended Scotch
    whisky
1 part Drambuie liqueur
Splash lime juice
Ice cubes

Shake with ice. Serve in a rocks glass.

Laser Disc

½ part Dewar's White Label Blended Scotch
   whisky
½ part Drambuie liqueur
½ part lemonade

Shake. Serve in a shot glass.

Loch Lomond

1 part Dewar's White Label Blended Scotch
   whisky
1 part Drambuie liqueur
½ part Martini & Rossi dry vermouth
Ice cubes
Lemon twist for garnish

Combine first three ingredients in a shaker half-filled with ice and shake well. Strain into a martini cocktail glass. Garnish with a lemon twist.

Mockingbird

1 ¼ oz. tequila
1 oz. fresh lime juice
2 tsp. Marie Brizard white crème de menthe
    liqueur
Ice cubes

Combine first three ingredients in a shaker and shake vigorously. Strain into a chilled cocktail glass with ice.

The Original Margarita

2 oz. tequila blanco
1 oz. Cointreau
¾ oz. fresh lime juice
Lime slice for garnish

Shake and strain into salt-rimmed margarita glass. Garnish with a lime slice.

The Pegu

1 ½ oz. gin
¾ oz. Cointreau
¾ oz. fresh lime juice
Dash Angostura bitters
Ice cubes

Shake and strain into a chilled martini glass.

Pink Squirrel

3 oz. vanilla ice cream
1 oz. Marie Brizard wild strawberry liqueur
½ oz. Marie Brizard white crème de cacao
   liqueur

Blend.

Santa Sobieski

1 ½ oz. Sobieski vodka
1 oz. Marie Brizard green crème de menthe
   liqueur
Maraschino cherry for garnish

Layer in a shot glass. Top with a maraschino
cherry.

Scottish Iced Tea

Freshly brewed unsweetened tea, iced
2 oz. Drambuie liqueur
Lemon slice or mint sprig for garnish

In a tall glass of freshly brewed unsweetened
iced tea, add Drambuie liqueur. Garnish with
lemon or a sprig of mint.

Sidecar

1 ½ oz. vodka
1 oz. Cointreau
1 oz. cranberry juice
¾ oz. fresh lime juice
Ice cubes
Coarse sugar for rim

Shake first four ingredients with ice. Strain into a chilled sugar-rimmed martini glass.

Singapore Sling

4 oz. pineapple juice
1 oz. gin
½ oz. cherry brandy
½ oz. fresh lime juice
¼ oz. Benedictine
¼ oz. Cointreau
¼ oz. grenadine syrup
Dash Angostura bitters
Ice cubes

Shake all ingredients well. Strain into a Collins glass.

S.O.B.

1 ½ oz. Sobieski vodka
½ oz. Marie Brizard Blackberry Cream liqueur
Ice cubes

Shake first two ingredients with ice and serve over ice or as a shot.

S.O.B. Sister

1 oz. Sobieski vodka
½ oz. Marie Brizard Anisette liqueur
½ oz. Marie Brizard blue curaçao liqueur

Shake with ice. Serve as a shot.

Sunkiss

2 ½ oz. pineapple juice
2 oz. Cointreau
1 ½ oz. yellow grapefruit juice
Ice cubes

Pour first three ingredients into a long drink glass over ice and stir.

White Cosmopolitan

1 oz. vodka
1 oz. white cranberry juice
½ oz. Cointreau
½ oz. fresh lemon juice

Shake and strain into a chilled martini glass.

White Lady

2 oz. gin
1 oz. Cointreau
½ oz. fresh lemon juice

Shake and strain into a chilled martini glass.

CREAMS

After Eight

½ oz. Baileys Irish cream
½ oz. coffee brandy
½ oz. green crème de menthe

After Five

1 oz. Carolans Irish cream
1 oz. peppermint schnapps
½ oz. Kahlúa

Amarula Brandy and Cream

1 oz. brandy
1 oz. fresh heavy cream
½ oz. Amarula Marula fruit cream
Chocolate shavings for garnish

Place all ingredients into shaker with ice and strain into a glass. Garnish with chocolate shavings.

Amarula Coffee

1 oz. hot coffee
1 oz. Amarula cream
Grated milk chocolate for garnish

Pour hot coffee into a cup and top with Amarula cream. Garnish with grated milk chocolate.

Amarula French Toast

1 ½ oz. Amarula Marula fruit cream
½ oz. Appleton rum, preferably amber or dark
½ oz. milk
Ground cinnamon for garnish
Cinnamon stick for garnish

Stir first three ingredients. Garnish with ground cinnamon and a cinnamon stick.

Avalanche

1 ½ oz. Carolans Irish cream
1 scoop vanilla ice cream
Splash cold milk

Blend.

Baileys B-52

Baileys Irish cream
Kahlúa
Orange liqueur

Layer equal parts of each in a shot glass.

Baileys Chocolate-Covered Cherry

½ oz. Baileys Irish cream
½ oz. grenadine
½ oz. Kahlúa
Maraschino cherry for garnish

Baileys Eggnog

2 cups milk
2 oz. Baileys Irish cream
1 oz. Irish whiskey
1 medium egg
Grated nutmeg for garnish

Shake with ice. Pour into 2 martini glasses.
Garnish both with grated nutmeg.

Beam Me Up, Scotty

Carolans Irish cream
Kahlúa
Crème de banana

Mix equal parts of each.

Café Vermeer

3 parts fresh hot coffee
1 part Vermeer Dutch Chocolate Cream
   liqueur
Whipped cream for top
Shaved chocolate for garnish

Top with whipped cream and shaved chocolate.

Carolans' Concerto Coffee

Carolans Irish cream
Tia Maria

Stir together equal parts of each.

Cinnamon Toast

1 ½ oz. Amarula Marula fruit cream liqueur
½ oz. cinnamon-flavored spirit
Coca-Cola to top
Ground cinnamon for garnish
Cinnamon stick for garnish

Shake. Splash Coke on top of mixture. Garnish with a sprinkle of ground cinnamon and a cinnamon stick.

Devil Mint

2 parts Vermeer Dutch Chocolate Cream
    liqueur
1 part white crème de menthe

Dirty Nelly

1 oz. Carolans Irish cream
1 oz. Tullamore Dew

Shake.

Duck Fart

1 oz. Kahlúa
1 oz. Carolans Irish cream
¼ oz. Canadian Club

Layer first Kahlúa, then Carolans Irish cream. Top with Canadian Club.

Easy Eggnog

1 qt. dairy eggnog
1 cup Southern Comfort bourbon
Ground nutmeg for dusting

Chill ingredients. Combine and blend in punch bowl. Dust with nutmeg.

French Cream

4 oz. ice cubes
2 oz. half-and-half
1 ½ oz. Baileys Irish cream
½ oz. Chambord

Blend for 30 seconds.

Italian Toasted Almond

1 part amaretto
1 part cream
1 part Glacier vodka
1 part illy Espresso liqueur

Shake.

Luck of the Irish

2 parts Carolans Irish cream
2 parts Tullamore Dew Irish whiskey
1 part Irish Mist

Shake.

Malibu Slide

Baileys Irish cream
Kahlúa
Malibu Original Caribbean rum

Blend equal parts of each.

Mint Kiss

3 oz. coffee
2 oz. Baileys Irish cream
1 oz. Rumple Minze peppermint schnapps
Fresh whipped cream to top

Top with fresh whipped cream.

Mudslide

1 oz. Baileys Irish cream
1 oz. Kahlúa
1 oz. Smirnoff vodka

Mix and pour. Serve straight up or on the rocks.

Nutty Irishman

1 part Carolans Irish cream
1 part Frangelico liqueur
Ice cubes

Shake first two ingredients well and pour over ice.

Oatmeal Cookie

Baileys Irish cream
Butterscotch schnapps
Goldschlager Cinnamon schnapps

Mix equal parts.

Southern Alexander

1 ½ oz. crème de cacao
1 ½ oz. Southern Comfort bourbon
1 cup ice cubes

Blend.

Tarzan O'Reilly

1 oz. Carolans Irish cream
1 oz. crème de banana
1 oz. FRïS Vodka

Stir.

Tootsie Roll

1 oz. root beer schnapps
½ oz. Baileys Irish cream

Poor root beer schnapps into a shot glass. Top with Baileys Irish cream.

Tuaca Creamsicle

1 oz. cream
1 oz. orange juice
1 oz. TUACA Vanilla Citrus liqueur
1 oz. vanilla-flavored vodka

Shake.

Tuaca on Heaven's Door

½ oz. hazelnut liqueur
½ oz. Irish Cream liqueur
½ oz. TUACA Vanilla Citrus liqueur
½ oz. vanilla-flavored vodka
Peppermint patty for garnish

Shake. Garnish with peppermint patty.

Ultimate Irish Coffee

3 oz. hot coffee
2 oz. Carolans Irish cream

White Russian

1 ½ parts Kahlúa
1 part Stolichnaya vodka
Ice cubes
1 ½ parts heavy cream for top

Pour first two ingredients over ice. Top with the cream.

Wild Rover

1 part Carolans Irish cream
1 part Irish Mist
Ice cubes

Serve on the rocks.

GIN

The Gin Martini

2 oz. gin
Dash Martini & Rossi extra dry vermouth
Lemon twist or olive for garnish

Stir in a cocktail shaker with ice. Strain and serve straight up in a cocktail glass or on the rocks. Add lemon twist or olive.

 MANY CUSTOMERS AND BARTENDERS AGREE THAT SHAKING WILL RUIN A MARTINI BECAUSE OF THE SLIGHT TASTE OF THE METAL FROM THE SHAKER. USE YOUR OWN JUDGMENT!

• • •

Put a spin on the Martini with these variations.

Alizé
Replace Martini & Rossi extra dry vermouth with Alizé.

Alizé Passionate
Replace Martini & Rossi extra dry vermouth with Alizé and dash of cranberry juice.

Cornet
Replace Martini & Rossi extra dry vermouth with port wine.

Dewey
Add a dash of orange bitters.

Dillatini
Garnish with a Dilly Bean (try to find one).

Elegant
Add a dash of Grand Marnier.

Fascinator
Add a dash of Pernod and a sprig of mint.

Gibson
Add a pickled cocktail onion.

Gimlet
Replace Martini & Rossi extra dry vermouth with lime juice. Garnish with lime twist.

Gypsy
Add a maraschino cherry.

Homestead
Muddle an orange slice in the glass.

Italian
Replace the Martini & Rossi extra dry vermouth with amaretto.

Jackson
Replace the Martini & Rossi extra dry vermouth with Dubonnet and a dash of bitters.

Ladies' Choice
Add ¼ oz. kummel.

Lone Tree
Add a dash of lemon juice.

Mickey Finn
Add a splash of white crème de menthe, and garnish with a sprig of mint.

Naked Martini
Just gin.

Naval Cocktail
Replace Martini & Rossi extra dry vermouth with Martini & Rossi Rosso sweet vermouth; add a cocktail onion and a twist.

Orangetini
Add a splash of triple sec and an orange peel twist.

Perfection
Replace the Martini & Rossi extra dry vermouth with Martini & Rossi Rosso sweet vermouth.

Queen Elizabeth
Add a splash of Benedictine.

Red Passion
Replace the Martini & Rossi extra dry vermouth with Alizé Red Passion.

Richmond
Replace the Martini & Rossi extra dry vermouth with Lillet, and add a twist of lemon.

Rosa
Add cherry brandy.

Rosalind Russell
Replace the Martini & Rossi extra dry vermouth with aquavit.

Roselyn
Add lime juice, grenadine, and a lemon twist.

Rouge
Add a dash of Chambord.

Saketini
Replace the Martini & Rossi extra dry vermouth with sake.

Silver Bullet
Float Cutty Sark on top.

Sour Kisses
Add egg white; shake.

Trinity (aka Trio)
Replace half of the Martini & Rossi extra dry vermouth plaza with Martini & Rossi Rosso sweet vermouth. Equal parts of vermouth and gin.

Velocity
Add an orange slice and shake.

Wallick
Add a dash of orange curaçao.

Warden
Add a dash of Pernod.

Alexander Cocktail

1 oz. cream
1 oz. gin
1 oz. white crème de cacao
Grated nutmeg for garnish

Shake. Garnish with the nutmeg.

Alexander's Sister

1 oz. cream
1 oz. crème de menthe
1 oz. dry gin

Shake and strain.

Alfonso Special

1 ½ oz. triple sec
¾ oz. gin
¾ oz. Martini & Rossi dry vermouth
4 dashes Martini & Rossi Rosso sweet
    vermouth
Dash Angostura bitters

Stir or shake.

Angel Face

1 oz. apple brandy
1 oz. apricot brandy
1 oz. gin

Shake.

Authentic Gin Martini

2 oz. gin
½ oz. dry vermouth
Ice cubes
Green or black olive for garnish

Shake first two ingredients well with ice. Strain into martini glass. Garnish with an olive.

Beauty Spot

1 ½ oz. gin
2 tsp. white crème de cacao
½ tsp. grenadine

Shake and strain.

Beekman Place

2 oz. sloe gin
1 oz. gin
1 oz. grenadine
1 tsp. lemon juice

Shake.

Belmont Cocktail

2 oz. gin
¾ oz. cream
1 tsp. grenadine

Shake.

Bitch on Wheels

2 oz. Gordon's gin
½ oz. extra dry vermouth
¼ oz. Pernod
¼ oz. white crème de menthe
Ice cubes

Shake and strain into a chilled martini glass.

Black Martini

2 ½ oz. Gordon's gin
Splash Chambord

Blue Canary

¾ oz. gin
3 tbsp. grapefruit juice
1 tbsp. blue curaçao
Ice cubes
Crushed ice
Mint sprig for garnish

Combine first three ingredients with ice cubes in mixing glass and stir gently. Strain into chilled cocktail glass filled with crushed ice. Garnish with mint.

Cosmopolitan (Gin)

1 ½ oz. gin
¼ oz. triple sec
2 dashes cranberry juice
2 dashes lime juice
Ice cubes
Lemon twist for garnish

Shake vigorously over ice and strain into a chilled martini glass. Twist a lemon peel over the drink and drop into the glass.

Cucumber Cooler

1 ½ parts Hendrick's gin
¾ part St. Germain Elderflower liqueur
¾ part fresh lime juice
5 mint leaves
¼ part simple syrup
Soda water
Cucumber slice for garnish

Place all ingredients but soda water in a long glass. Muddle gently. Add ice and top with soda water. Add a cucumber garnish.

Cucumber Martini

2 ½ parts Hendrick's gin
½ part dry vermouth
Cucumber slice for garnish

Stir Hendrick's gin and vermouth in a mixing glass with ice. Strain into a chilled martini glass. Finish with a cucumber garnish.

Emerald Isle Cocktail

2 oz. gin
1 tsp. green crème de menthe
2 dashes bitters
Ice cubes

Stir and strain into a cocktail glass.

Flamingo

2 oz. pineapple juice
1 oz. cream of coconut
1 oz. gin
1 oz. sweet-and-sour mix

Blend together with cracked ice until smooth.
Strain and serve in a chilled glass.

French 75

2 oz. gin
Juice 1 lemon
2 tsp. sugar
Ice cubes
Chilled champagne to fill
Lemon or orange slice for garnish
Maraschino cherry for garnish

Stir first three ingredients in a Collins glass.
Then add ice cubes and fill with champagne.
Garnish with a lemon or orange slice and a mara-
schino cherry.

Gimlet

1 ¼ oz. gin
¾ oz. lime juice
Ice cubes
Lime slice for garnish

Pour first two ingredients over ice. Stir and strain into chilled martini glass. Garnish with the lime slice.

Gin and Passion

Coarse sugar for rim
1 oz. Bulldog gin
1 oz. passion fruit liqueur
Ice cubes

Rim shot glass with sugar. Shake ingredients and strain into shot glass.

Gin Surfer

1 ½ oz. Bulldog gin
½ oz. blue curaçao
Ice cubes

Shake ingredients and strain into a shot glass.

Gloom Raiser

2 ½ oz. gin
½ oz. dry vermouth
2 dashes grenadine
2 dashes Pernod

Stir and strain.

Golden Dawn

1 ½ oz. gin
¾ oz. apricot brandy
¾ oz. orange juice

Shake and strain.

Golf Cocktail

2 oz. gin
1 oz. Martini & Rossi extra dry vermouth
2 dashes Angostura bitters

Stir and strain.

Green Devil

1 ½ oz. gin
½ oz. lime juice
2 tsp. green crème de menthe
Mint leaves for garnish

Shake and strain. Garnish with mint leaves.

Gypsy Life

2 oz. gin
1 oz. Benedictine
1-2 dashes Angostura bitters

Shake and strain.

Hasty Cocktail

1 ½ oz. gin
¾ oz. dry vermouth
¼ tsp. Pernod
3 dashes grenadine

Shake and strain.

Hendrick's Breeze

1 ½ parts Hendrick's gin
2 parts white cranberry juice
Splash Fresca
Ice cubes
Lemon wheel for garnish
Orange wheel for garnish

Build over ice in a tall glass. Garnish with lemon and orange wheels.

Hey Bulldog!

2 oz. Bulldog gin
1 oz. Chambord
½ oz. peppermint schnapps
7-Up to top

Combine all ingredients except 7-Up in a highball glass and stir. Top with 7-Up.

Highball

2 oz. gin
Ice cubes
Ginger ale or club soda to fill
Lemon twist for garnish (optional)

Pour the gin into a highball glass over ice cubes, fill with ginger ale or club soda, and stir.

Last Tango

1 ½ oz. gin
1 oz. orange juice
½ oz. triple sec

Shake and strain.

The Last Word

¾ oz. green chartreuse
¾ oz. Hendrick's gin
¾ oz. maraschino liqueur
¾ oz. fresh lime juice

Shake all ingredients briefly over ice and serve in an ice-filled rocks glass. Garnish with a smile.

Leave-It-to-Me Cocktail

1 oz. gin
½ oz. apricot brandy
½ oz. Martini & Rossi extra dry vermouth
2 dashes lemon juice
Dash grenadine

Shake and strain.

Lemoneater

2 oz. gin
Ice cubes
Lemonade to fill

Add the gin to a glass filled with ice and add lemonade.

Little Devil Cocktail

1 oz. Bacardi rum
1 oz. gin
¾ oz. triple sec
Juice ¼ lemon

Shake and strain.

London Cider

4 oz. apple cider
2 oz. Bulldog gin
Apple slice for garnish

Combine ingredients in a rocks glass with ice.
Garnish with apple slice.

London Lemonade

4 oz. fresh lemonade
2 oz. Bulldog gin
Ice cubes
Lemon wedge for garnish

Combine first two ingredients in a cocktail glass
with ice. Garnish with lemon wedge.

London Light

2 oz. Bulldog gin
1 oz. pomegranate juice
½ oz. grapefruit juice
Club soda to top
Strawberry slice for garnish

Combine gin, pomegranate juice, and grapefruit
juice in a cocktail glass. Top with club soda.
Garnish with a strawberry slice.

Maiden's Prayer

1 ½ oz. gin
1 ½ oz. triple sec
½ oz. lemon juice

Shake and strain.

Meadow Mule

1 ½ parts Hendrick's gin
1 part apple juice
½ part elderflower cordial
Ice cubes
Ginger ale
Cucumber spear for garnish

Build ingredients over ice in a long glass and finish with ginger ale. Garnish with the cucumber.

Moonshot

3 oz. clam juice
1 ¼ oz. gin
Dash red pepper sauce
Ice cubes

Stir over ice cubes.

Napoleon

1 ¼ oz. gin
½ oz. Dubonnet Rouge
½ oz. triple sec
Ice cubes

Combine first three ingredients with ice in a mixing glass. Stir well and strain into a cocktail glass.

Negroni

¾ oz. Campari
¾ oz. gin
¾ oz. Martini & Rossi Rosso sweet vermouth
Lemon twist for garnish

Stir with ice in an aperitif glass; twist lemon peel over drink and drop it into the glass. Garnish with the lemon twist.

Orange Blossom Cocktail

2 oz. gin
1 oz. orange juice
¼ tsp. sugar (optional)

Shake and strain.

Orange Burst

1 ½ parts Hendrick's gin
¾ part fresh orange juice
Splash Angostura bitters
Lemon wedge
Ice cubes
Ginger ale
Soda water

In a long glass combine the first three ingredients. Squeeze a wedge of lemon and drop it into the drink. Add ice. Top with equal parts ginger ale and soda water and give a good stir.

Orient Express

1 oz. brandy
1 oz. gin
1 oz. Maker's Mark bourbon

Stir and strain.

Parisian

1 oz. crème de cassis
1 oz. Martini & Rossi extra dry vermouth
1 oz. gin

Shake and strain.

Park Avenue

2 oz. gin
1 oz. Martini & Rossi Rosso sweet vermouth
1 oz. pineapple juice
1–2 dashes curaçao (optional)

Shake and strain.

Pink Lady

3 oz. half-and-half
1 ¼ oz. gin
2 tsp. grenadine

Shake with ice and strain into a cocktail glass or serve on the rocks.

Pink Pussycat

2 oz. grapefruit juice
2 oz. pineapple juice
1 ½ oz. gin
Dash grenadine
Ice cubes

Pour over rocks in a tall glass and stir.

Plumdog Millionaire

2 oz. Bulldog gin
1 oz. lavender soda
1 oz. Japanese plum wine
Ice cubes
Lavender sugar for rim
Half-wheel slice black plum for garnish

Combine first three ingredients and stir over ice
then strain. Serve in a martini glass with a rim
of lavender sugar and a black plum half wheel
for garnish.

Pollyanna Cocktail

2 oz. gin
⅔ oz. sweet vermouth
½ tsp. grenadine
3 slices orange
3 slices pineapple

Shake and strain.

Polo

1 ¼ oz. gin
1 oz. grapefruit juice to fill
1 oz. orange juice to fill

Pour the gin in a tall glass with ice. Fill with equal parts grapefruit juice and orange juice.

Red Coat

5 oz. cranberry juice
1 ½ oz. gin
Ice cubes

Serve in a tall glass over ice.

Red Ruby

1 ½ oz. gin
½ oz. grenadine
½ oz. Martini & Rossi extra dry vermouth
Ice cubes

Combine first three ingredients in a mixing glass half filled with ice cubes, and stir well. Strain into a cocktail glass.

Rickey

2 oz. gin
Juice ½ lime
Chilled club soda to fill
Maraschino cherry for garnish

Stir and garnish with the cherry.

Salty Dog

Coarse salt for rim (optional)
1 ¼ oz. gin
Ice cubes
3 oz. grapefruit juice

Wet rim of tall glass with juice or water and dip into salt to coat (optional). Pour gin over ice, fill with grapefruit juice, and stir.

Seagram's Gin Gimlet

1 ¼ oz. Seagram's gin
¾ oz. lime juice
Lime slice for garnish

Pour over ice in a cocktail glass. Stir. Garnish with a slice of lime.

Sidecar in Bombay

1 oz. Bombay Sapphire gin
¼ oz. Grand Marnier
¼ oz. lemon juice
Ice cubes

Shake and serve on the rocks or up in a sugar-rimmed glass.

Singapore Sling

1 ½ oz. gin
½ oz. cherry brandy
½ oz. lemon juice
1 tsp. grenadine
Chilled club soda to fill
Lemon or lime slice for garnish
Maraschino cherry for garnish

Mix first four ingredients and top with club soda. Garnish with lemon or lime slice and maraschino cherry.

Slim Gin

¼ oz. gin
Diet soda to fill

In a tall glass filled with ice and your favorite diet soda.

Sling

2 oz. gin
1 oz. cherry brandy
Juice ½ lemon
1 tsp. sugar
1 tsp. water
Lemon twist for garnish

Shake and strain. Garnish with the lemon twist.

Smooth Melody

Ice cubes
1 oz. gin
1 oz. orange juice
Ginger ale to fill
Maraschino cherry for garnish

Fill a glass with ice, add the gin and juice, fill with ginger ale, and stir. Garnish with the cherry.

Spiked Mojito

3 sprigs fresh mint, chopped
2 lime slices
1 oz. simple syrup
2 oz. Bulldog gin
1 ½ oz. lychee juice
Club soda to top

Muddle mint and lime slices with simple syrup. Add Bulldog gin and lychee juice. Shake with ice. Top with club soda. Serve in an old-fashioned glass.

Stinger (Gin)

1 oz. gin
¼ oz. white crème de menthe
Ice cubes

Stir well on the rocks.

Strawberries and Cream

2 oz. Bulldog gin
1 oz. strawberry liqueur
1 oz. white crème de cacao
½ oz. half-and-half
Strawberry for garnish
Cocoa powder for garnish

Shake all ingredients with ice and strain. Garnish with a strawberry and cocoa powder.

Tom Collins

2 oz. gin
¾ oz. lemon juice
½ oz. sugar syrup
Ice cubes
Club soda to fill
Maraschino cherry for garnish
Lemon slice for garnish

Stir the first four ingredients well in a Collins glass, and fill with club soda. Garnish with the cherry and lemon slice.

Twisted Tonic

1 ¼ oz. Seagram's Lime Twisted gin
Ice cubes
6 oz. tonic water

Pour gin over ice in a tall glass. Fill with tonic water. Stir to blend.

Union Jack

1 ½ oz. gin
½ oz. sloe gin
1 tsp. grenadine

Shake and strain.

Unusual Negroni

1 part Aperol liqueur
1 part Hendrick's gin
1 part Lillet Blanc
Orange twist for garnish

Combine ingredients and shake well with ice. Serve up and garnish with an orange twist.

The Yellow Fellow

1 oz. gin
¼ oz. yellow Chartreuse

Shake and strain into a cocktail glass.

IRISH WHISKEY

Brainstorm

1 ¾ oz. Tullamore Dew Irish whiskey
¼ oz. Martini & Rossi dry vermouth
Dash Benedictine
Orange twist for garnish

Stir and strain into a cocktail glass. Garnish with
the orange twist.

Emerald Isle

2 scoops vanilla ice cream
2 oz. Tullamore Dew Irish whiskey
¼ oz. green crème de menthe
2 oz. club soda to fill

Blend the first three ingredients, add soda water,
and stir.

Grit Cocktail

1 oz. Martini & Rossi sweet vermouth
1 oz. Tullamore Dew Irish whiskey

Shake and strain into a cocktail glass.

Hot Irish

1 slice fresh lemon
4 cloves
1–2 tsp. superfine sugar
Pinch cinnamon or cinnamon stick
3–4 oz. boiling water
1 ¼ oz. Tullamore Dew Irish whiskey

Stud the lemon slice with cloves. Put the lemon slice, sugar, and cinnamon into a stemmed glass. Add the boiling water and whiskey. Stir and serve.

Irish Coffee

4 oz. hot coffee
2 oz. Tullamore Dew Irish whiskey
Superfine sugar to taste
¼ oz. Carolans Irish cream

Pour the coffee into a warm stemmed glass. Add Irish whiskey and sugar. Stir well. Float the Carolans Irish cream.

Irish Cooler

1 ¼ oz. Tullamore Dew Irish whiskey
Ice cubes
6 oz. club soda
Lemon peel spiral for garnish

Pour the Tullamore Dew into a highball glass over ice cubes. Top with soda and stir. Garnish with a lemon peel spiral.

Irish Cow

8 oz. hot milk
1 ½ oz. Tullamore Dew Irish whiskey
1 tsp. superfine sugar

Pour the milk into a glass; add the whiskey and sugar. Stir well.

Irish Cresta

1 oz. Tullamore Dew Irish whiskey
1 egg white
2 tsp. Irish Mist
2 tsp. orange juice
Ice cubes

Combine with ice. Shake REALLY well. Pour into a rocks glass and serve.

Irish Fizz

2 oz. Tullamore Dew Irish whiskey
1 ½ tsp. lemon juice
1 tsp. triple sec
½ tsp. superfine sugar
Ice cubes
Club soda to fill

Combine the first four ingredients with ice and shake. Strain and serve in a rocks glass. Top with club soda.

Irish Whiskey Cooler

4 oz. club soda
2 oz. Tullamore Dew Irish whiskey
Dash Angostura bitters
Lemon rind for garnish

Serve in a tall glass. Garnish with the lemon rind.

Irish Whiskey Sour

2 oz. Tullamore Dew Irish whiskey
2 oz. lemon juice
1 bar spoon superfine sugar
Maraschino cherry for garnish
Orange slice for garnish

Shake and strain into a sour glass or serve on the rocks. Garnish with the cherry and orange slice.

Kerry Cooler

1 oz. Tullamore Dew Irish whiskey
½ oz. sherry
1 ¼ tbsp. crème de almond
1 ¼ tbsp. sweet-and-sour mix
Ice cubes
Club soda
Lemon slice for garnish

Combine first four ingredients with ice. Shake well. Strain and top with club soda. Garnish with the lemon slice.

Let's Dew Coffee

6 oz. coffee
1 ½ oz. Tullamore Dew Irish whiskey
Whipped cream for garnish

Pour the whiskey into the hot mug of coffee. Top with the whipped cream.

Luck of the Irish

1 oz. Carolans Irish cream
1 oz. Tullamore Dew Irish whiskey
½ oz. Irish Mist Irish whiskey liqueur
Ice cubes

Shake and serve on the rocks.

Misty Dew

1 oz. Irish Mist Irish whiskey liqueur
1 oz. Tullamore Dew Irish whiskey
Ice cubes

Serve over ice in a rocks glass.

New Castle's Best

1 ¼ oz. Tullamore Dew Irish whiskey
½ oz. Irish Mist Irish whiskey liqueur
Few drops white crème de cacao
Ice cubes

Shake first three ingredients with ice. Serve straight up or on the rocks.

Paddy Cocktail

¾ oz. Martini & Rossi Rosso sweet vermouth
¾ oz. Tullamore Dew Irish whiskey
2 dashes bitters

Combine with ice and shake. Strain into an old-fashioned glass with ice.

Red Devil

2 oz. Tullamore Dew Irish whiskey
1 ½ oz. clam juice
1 ½ oz. tomato juice
1 tsp. lime juice
Few drops Worcestershire sauce
Pinch pepper
Ice cubes

Combine all ingredients and shake gently. Strain and serve straight up.

Ring of Kerry

1 ½ oz. Tullamore Dew Irish whiskey
1 oz. Carolans Irish cream
½ oz. Kahlúa
Cracked ice
1 tsp. shaved chocolate for garnish

Mix first three ingredients with cracked ice in a shaker or blender. Strain into a chilled cocktail glass. Garnish with shaved chocolate.

Tipperary

¾ oz. Martini & Rossi Rosso sweet vermouth
¾ oz. Tullamore Dew Irish whiskey
1 tbsp. green Chartreuse

Combine with ice and shake well. Strain into an old-fashioned glass with ice.

Tullamore Yankee Dew

Generous portion of Tullamore Dew over ice.

007 Martini

Extra dry vermouth
1 oz. Gordon's Special Dry London gin
1 oz. Gordon's vodka
½ oz. Lillet
Lemon twist for garnish

Rinse a glass with extra dry vermouth. Shake gin, vodka, and Lillet with ice and strain into the glass. Garnish with the lemon twist.

24-Karat Martini

2 ½ oz. Ketel One vodka
Spicy baby carrot for garnish

Serve straight up or over ice. Garnish with the spicy baby carrot.

360 Apple Tree Hugger

1 oz. 360 vodka
1 oz. sour apple schnapps
1 oz. sweet-and-sour mix
Ice cubes

Shake and strain into a martini glass.

360 Double Chocolate Raspberry

2 oz. 360 Double Chocolate
1 oz. sweet-and-sour mix
½ oz. agave nectar
¼ oz. raspberry liqueur
5 raspberries
Ice cubes
Splash lemon-lime soda

Shake first five ingredients with ice, and strain into a martini glass. Add a splash of lemon-lime soda.

Absolutly Fabulous Martini

1 ¼ oz. Absolut Citron vodka
1 ¼ oz. Absolut Kurant vodka
Ice cubes
Lemon twist for garnish

Shake and strain into a chilled martini glass. Garnish with the lemon twist.

 THE MARTINI CLUB, ATLANTA, GA

Acropolis Martini

1 ¾ oz. Smirnoff vodka
¼ oz. Ouzo 12
Ice cubes
Black olive for garnish

Shake and strain into a glass. Garnish with the black olive.

Algonquin Martini

2 oz. blended whiskey
1 oz. Martini & Rossi extra dry vermouth
1 oz. unsweetened pineapple juice

Shake with ice and strain into a chilled cocktail glass or serve over ice in an old-fashioned glass.

 ALGONQUIN HOTEL, NEW YORK, NY

Angel Martini

1 ½ oz. Ketel One vodka
½ oz. Frangelico liqueur
Ice cubes

Shake and strain into a chilled martini glass.

Antini Martini

2 oz. Stolichnaya vodka
½ oz. Lillet Rouge
Ice cubes
Burnt orange twist for garnish

Shake and strain into a chilled martini glass. Garnish with the burnt orange twist. (Hold twist between two hands and twist over fire until it flames from essence of orange.)

Apple Martini

1 ½ oz. Glacier vodka
½ oz. Schoenauer Apfel schnapps
Ice cubes
Dash cinnamon
Apple slice for garnish

Shake and strain into a chilled martini glass. Garnish with cinnamon and an apple slice.

Bacardi Dry Martini

2 oz. Bacardi rum
½ oz. Martini & Rossi extra dry vermouth
Ice cubes

Shake and strain into a chilled martini glass.

Ballet Russe

2 oz. Stolichnaya vodka
¼ oz. Chambord
¼ oz. sour mix
Ice cubes

Shake and strain into a chilled martini glass.

 THE DINER ON SYCAMORE, CINCINNATI, OH

A Bally Good Martini

2 oz. Bombay Sapphire gin
⅛ oz. Grand Marnier
⅛ oz. dry vermouth
Ice cubes
Orange twist for garnish

Shake and strain into a chilled martini glass. Garnish with the orange twist.

 BALLY'S, LAS VEGAS, NV

Bambou's Limon Martini

2 oz. Bacardi Limón rum
1 oz. Midori Melon liqueur
½ oz. Martini & Rossi extra dry vermouth
Lemon twist for garnish

 REEBOK SPORTS CLUB, NEW YORK, NY

Banzai Martini

⅛ oz. Martini & Rossi extra dry vermouth
2 ¾ oz. SKYY vodka
¼ oz. sake
Japanese pickled plum and shiso for garnish

Rinse glass with Martini & Rossi extra dry vermouth. Shake vodka and sake. Garnish with the Japanese pickled plum and shiso.

 BETELNUT, SAN FRANCISCO, CA

Barbarella

2 oz. vodka
Splash Martini & Rossi extra dry vermouth
Gorgonzola-stuffed olives for garnish

 WOLFGANG PUCK EXPRESS, WALT DISNEY WORLD RESORT, FL

Barbed Wire

2 ½ oz. vodka
¼ oz. Martini & Rossi Rosso sweet vermouth
Splash Chambord
Splash Pernod
Ice cubes
Maraschino cherry for garnish

Shake first four ingredients with ice. Strain into a martini glass. Top with maraschino cherry.

 HARRIS' SAN FRANCISCO STEAKHOUSE, SAN FRANCISCO, CA

Becco's Martini

1 ½ oz. Campari
1 ½ oz. Stolichnaya Ohranj vodka
½ oz. Martini & Rossi Rosso sweet vermouth
Orange peel for garnish

 REEBOK SPORTS CLUB, NEW YORK, NY

Bellini Martini

2 ½ oz. Stolichnaya vodka
½ oz. fresh white peach purée
Ice cubes
Lemon zest for garnish

Shake and strain into a chilled martini glass. Serve straight up or on the rocks. Garnish with the lemon zest.

Belvedere Strawberry Mint Martini

2 fresh strawberries (plus 1 for garnish)
4 mint leaves (plus 1 for garnish)
½ oz. fresh lemon juice
½ oz. simple syrup
2 oz. Belvedere vodka
Ice cubes

Muddle strawberries and mint with lemon juice and simple syrup. Add Belvedere. Shake with ice. Strain into a chilled martini glass. Garnish with the strawberry and mint leaf.

 KATIE STEVENS. LAFORCE + STEVENS

A Bentley Martini

2 oz. Calvados
1 oz. sweet vermouth
Lemon twist for garnish

Shake with ice and strain into a chilled martini
glass. Serve straight up. Garnish with the lemon
twist.

 TIM WORSTALL, SAN LUIS OBISPO, CA

Black Eyed "P"

3 oz. Absolut Peppar vodka
Black olives for garnish

Shake with ice and strain into a chilled martini
glass. Serve on the rocks or straight up. Garnish
with the olives.

 CECILIA'S, BRECKENRIDGE, CO

Black Jack Martini

2 oz. Jack Daniel's Tennessee whiskey
¼ oz. sweet vermouth
Dash Angostura bitters
Maraschino cherry for garnish

Shake with ice and strain into a chilled martini
glass. Garnish with the maraschino cherry.

Black Martini

1 ½ oz. Absolut Kurant vodka
Splash Chambord

Stir ingredients with ice and strain into a glass.
Serve straight up or on the rocks.

 CONTINENTAL CAFÉ, PHILADELPHIA, PA

Bleeding Heart Martini

Splash Campari
6 oz. Ketel One vodka
Black olive for garnish

Chill a bottle of Campari in freezer until it gets
syrupy. Wet and chill a cocktail glass in the freezer
as well. Swirl the vodka with ice, and strain into the
cocktail glass. Slowly pour the Campari around the
rim of the glass. Garnish with the black olive.

 THOMAS ROZYCKI, BLOOMSBURG, PA

Blonde Martini

2 ½ oz. Bombay Sapphire gin
¼ oz. Lillet Blonde

Shake with ice and strain into a chilled martini glass. Serve straight up or on the rocks.

 BRASSERIE JO, CHICAGO, IL

Carnival Martini

2 ½ oz. vodka
½ oz. orange juice
¼ oz. fresh lime juice

Shake with ice and strain into a chilled martini glass. Serve straight up or on the rocks.

 COCONUT GROVE, SAN FRANCISCO, CA

Ketel One Cosmopolitan Martini

2 oz. Ketel One vodka, chilled
¼ oz. Cointreau
Hint cranberry juice

Shake with ice and strain into a chilled martini glass. Serve on the rocks or straight up.

 DIVISION SIXTEEN, BOSTON, MA

Ying Martini

2 ½ oz. sake
½ oz. gin

Stir with ice and strain into a chilled martini glass.

 INAGIKU, NEW YORK, NY

POUSSE-CAFÉ

Everyone knows what proof means, but we're looking for specific gravity. For instance, crème de
cassis is the heaviest, or has the highest specific
gravity, at 1.1833. Anything above this will float.

NO.	PROOF	PRODUCT	SPECIFIC GRAVITY	COLOR
1	40	crème de cassis	1.1833	light brown
2	25	grenadine liqueur	1.1720	red
3	54	crème de cacao	1.1561	brown
4	48	hazelnut schnapps	1.1532	tawny
5	40	praline	1.1514	brown
6	54	crème de cacao white	1.1434	clear
7	56	crème de noyaux	1.1342	red

NO.	PROOF	PRODUCT	SPECIFIC GRAVITY	COLOR
8	48	licorice schnapps	1.1300	clear
9	54	chocolate cherry	1.1247	brown
10	56	crème de banana	1.1233	yellow
11	54	chocolate mint	1.1230	brown
12	48	blue curaçao	1.1215	blue
13	54	Swiss chocolate almond	1.1181	brown
14	60	crème de menthe white	1.1088	clear
15	60	crème de menthe green	1.1088	green
16	60	orange curaçao	1.1086	tawny
17	60	anisette white and red	1.0987	clear/red
18	48	crème de strawberry	1.0968	red
19	48	wild strawberry schnapps	1.0966	clear

NO.	PROOF	PRODUCT	SPECIFIC GRAVITY	COLOR
20	48	red hot schnapps	1.0927	red
21	60	triple sec	1.0922	clear
22	60	rock & rye	1.0887	yellow
23	40	cranberry cordial	1.0872	red
24	50	amaretto	1.0842	tawny
25	48	old-fashioned root beer schnapps	1.0828	tawny
26	84	sambuca	1.0813	clear
27	40	country melon schnapps	1.0828	tawny
28	70	coffee-flavored brandy	1.0794	brown
29	48	red raspberry schnapps	1.0752	clear
30	48	snappy apricot schnapps	1.0732	tawny
31	48	cinnamon schnapps	1.0732	red
32	48	spearmint schnapps	1.0732	clear

NO.	PROOF	PRODUCT	SPECIFIC GRAVITY	COLOR
33	60	shamrock schnapps	1.0617	green
34	60	peppermint schnapps	1.0615	clear
35	48	jubilee peach schnapps	1.0595	clear
36	70	raspberry-flavored brandy	1.0566	red
37	70	apricot-flavored brandy	1.0566	red
38	70	peach-flavored brandy	1.0547	tawny
39	70	cherry-flavored brandy	1.0542	red
40	70	blackberry-flavored brandy	1.0536	purple
41	90	peach schnapps	1.0534	clear
42	90	root beer schnapps	1.0441	brown
43	50	amaretto and cognac	1.0394	tawny

NO.	PROOF	PRODUCT	SPECIFIC GRAVITY	COLOR
44	90	cinnamon spice schnapps	1.0358	red
45	60	sloe gin	1.0241	red
46	70	ginger-flavored brandy	0.9979	light brown
47	90	Kirschwasser	0.9410	clear

Angel's Kiss

1 oz. dark crème de cacao
1 oz. cream

It's an Angel's Tit when you garnish with a cherry on a toothpick centered across the top.

Fourth of July

⅓ shot blue curaçao
⅓ shot grenadine
⅓ shot vodka

Gravure

Equal Parts:
Crème de cacao—brown
Grenadine—red

Irish Flag

Triple sec—clear
⅓ shot green crème de menthe
⅓ shot Grand Marnier
⅓ shot Irish Cream liqueur

Traffic Light

⅓ oz. crème de banana
⅓ oz. green crème de menthe
⅓ oz. sloe gin

RUMS

Afterburner

2 oz. J. Wray & Nephew White Overproof rum
½ oz. Kahlúa
½ oz. peppermint schnapps

Pour ingredients into a snifter glass. Swirl to mix.

Angostura Fuh So

1 oz. amaretto
1 oz. Angostura white rum
1 oz. heavy cream
Fresh cinnamon to taste
3–4 dashes Angostura aromatic bitters
½ oz. grenadine

Blend first five ingredients and layer on grenadine.

Angostura Royale

2 oz. Angostura 1919 rum
2 oz. pineapple juice
1 oz. Cointreau
½ oz. blue curaçao
3-4 dashes Angostura aromatic bitters
Lime wedges for garnish

Shake and garnish with lime wedges.

Angostura Stinger

1 oz. Angostura 1919 rum
1 oz. heavy cream
½ oz. white crème de cacao
¼ oz. white crème de menthe
Dash blue food coloring
304 dashes Angostura aromatic bitters
Maraschino cherries for garnish
Parsley snips for garnish

Shake and garnish with cherries and parsley
snips.

Apple Daiquiri

1 oz. apple schnapps
1 oz. light rum
½ oz. sweet-and-sour mix
Apple slice for garnish

Blend first three ingredients. Garnish with the apple slice.

Appleton Blue Lagoon

5 oz. lemonade
1 oz. blue curaçao
½ oz. Appleton Estate V/X Jamaica rum
Ice cubes
Lime wedge for garnish

Pour into a highball or Collins glass over ice and stir. Garnish with lime wedge.

Appleton Doctor Bird

½ lime
3 oz. pineapple juice
1 ½ oz. Appleton Estate V/X Jamaica rum
1 tsp. sugar
3 oz. ginger ale
Maraschino cherry for garnish
Pineapple wedge for garnish

Cut up the lime. Remove rind. Blend with pineapple juice, rum, and sugar and mix until smooth. Pour into a Collins or rocks glass, top with ginger ale, and garnish with the cherry and pineapple wedge.

Appleton Exotic Lady

½ lime
2 oz. pineapple juice
1 ½ oz. Appleton Estate V/X Jamaica rum
¼ oz. grenadine
1 tsp. granulated sugar
2 oz. ginger ale
Maraschino cherry for garnish
Pineapple wedge for garnish

Cut up lime and mix with pineapple juice, rum, grenadine, and sugar over ice. Strain into a martini glass. Top with ginger ale. Garnish with the cherry and pineapple wedge.

Appleton Jamaica Sunset

2 ½ oz. cranberry juice
1 ½ oz. Appleton Estate V/X Jamaica rum
3 ½ oz. orange juice
Orange wheel for garnish

Pour first two ingredients into a highball or
stemware glass over ice. Slowly add orange juice.
Garnish with orange wheel.

Assam Chai Punch

3 oz. chai tea
1 ½ oz. Pyrat Rum XO Reserve rum
1 oz. orange juice
1 oz. fresh sweet-and-sour mix
½ oz. Grand Marnier
Ice cubes
Orange twist for garnish
Mint sprig for garnish

Shake first five ingredients and strain over ice.
Garnish with orange twist and fresh mint sprig.

Bacardi and Coke (Cuba Libre)

1 ½ oz. Bacardi Gold rum
Ice cubes
Coca-Cola to fill
Generous squeeze of lime for garnish

Pour rum into a glass filled with ice. Fill with cola. Garnish with lime juice.

Bacardi Black Dirty Colada

2 oz. pineapple juice
1 ¼ oz. Bacardi black rum
1 oz. Coco Lopez Real Cream of Coconut

Blend.

Bacardi Blossom

1 ¼ oz. Bacardi light rum
1 oz. orange juice
½ oz. lemon juice
½ tsp. sugar
Ice cubes

Mix in a shaker or blender and strain into a cocktail glass.

Bacardi Cocktail

1 ¼ oz. Bacardi light rum
1 oz. lime juice
½ oz. grenadine
½ tsp. sugar
Ice cubes

Mix in a shaker or blender and strain into a chilled cocktail glass or serve on the rocks.

 THE NY SUPREME COURT RULED IN 1936 THAT A BACARDI COCKTAIL IS NOT A BACARDI COCKTAIL UNLESS IT'S MADE WITH BACARDI RUM.

Bacardi Daiquiri

1 ¼ oz. Bacardi light rum
½ oz. lemon juice
½ tsp. sugar
Ice cubes

Mix in a shaker or blender and strain into a chilled cocktail glass or serve on the rocks.

 THE ORIGINAL DAIQUIRI WAS MADE WITH BACARDI RUM IN 1896.

Bacardi Fizz

1 ¼ oz. Bacardi light rum
¼ oz. lemon juice
Ice cubes
¼ oz. grenadine
Club soda to fill

Pour the rum and lemon juice into a highball glass filled with ice. Add the grenadine and fill with soda.

Bacardi Grasshopper

1 oz. Bacardi light rum
½ oz. heavy cream
¼ oz. green crème de menthe
Ice cubes

Mix in a shaker or blender and strain into a cocktail glass.

Bacardi Hemingway

1 ½ oz. Bacardi light rum
Juice ½ lime
¼ oz. grapefruit juice
¼ oz. maraschino liqueur

Mix.

Bacardi Key Largo

2 oz. orange juice
1 ½ oz. Bacardi dark rum
1 ½ oz. Coco Lopez Real Cream of Coconut
Maraschino cherry for garnish

Garnish with a maraschino cherry.

Bacardi Mojito

12 mint leaves
½ lime
4 tsp. sugar
2 dashes Angostura bitters
Ice
1 ½ oz. Bacardi light-dry rum
Club soda to fill
Sprig of mint or lime wheel for garnish

Place the mint leaves and lime in a Collins glass.
Crush well with the back of a spoon. Add the
sugar and bitters. Fill glass with ice. Add the rum
and top with club soda. Stir well. Garnish with
the mint or lime wheel.

Bacardi Orange Daiquiri

1 ½ oz. Bacardi light rum
1 oz. orange juice
½ oz. lime or lemon juice
1 tsp. sugar
½ cup crushed ice

Blend all ingredients. Serve in a chilled cocktail glass.

Bacardi Peach Daiquiri

3 oz. Bacardi light rum
2 fresh peach halves, peeled (or 2 canned peach halves)
1 tsp. sugar (omit sugar if using canned peaches)
1 oz. lime or lemon juice
½ cup crushed ice

Blend. Serve in chilled cocktail glasses. Serves two.

 THIS IS THE OFFICIAL DRINK OF THE NATIONAL PEACH COUNCIL.

Bacardi Piña Colada

2 oz. unsweetened pineapple juice
1 ½ oz. Bacardi light or dark rum
1 oz. Coco Lopez Cream of Coconut

Blend with ½ cup ice or shake and serve over ice.

Bacardi Pink Squeeze

1 ½ oz. Bacardi light rum
Ice cubes
Pink lemonade to fill

Pour rum into a tall glass over ice and fill with pink lemonade.

Bacardi Rickey

½ lemon or lime
Ice cubes
1 ¼ oz. Bacardi light rum
Club soda to fill

Squeeze the lemon or lime into a tall glass filled with ice. Add the rum and fill with club soda.

Bacardi Rum Punch

1 oz. Bacardi light rum
¼ oz. white crème de menthe
Ice cubes
Milk or heavy cream

Pour the rum and white crème de menthe into a tall glass half-filled with ice. Fill with milk or cream.

Bacardi Select Calypso Coffee

1 ½ oz. Bacardi Select rum
¾ oz. dark crème de cacao
6 oz. fresh hot coffee
Whipped cream for garnish
Ground cinnamon for garnish

Mix ingredients in a coffee cup, and fill with hot black coffee. Garnish with whipped cream and ground cinnamon

Bacardi Select Eggnog

1 ¼ oz. Bacardi Select rum
1 egg
1 tsp. sugar
2 oz. milk
Grated nutmeg for garnish

Mix in a shaker and strain into a tall glass.
Sprinkle with nutmeg.

Bacardi Select Hot-Buttered Rum

1 ¼ oz. Bacardi Select rum
1 tsp. sugar
½ tsp. butter
4 whole cloves

Mix the rum, sugar, butter, and cloves in a mug.
Fill with boiling water and stir.

Bacardi Sour

1 ¼ oz. Bacardi Gold rum
1 oz. lemon juice
½ tsp. sugar
Ice cubes
Maraschino cherry for garnish
Orange half for garnish

Mix first three ingredients in a shaker with ice and strain into a sour glass. Garnish with the cherry and orange half.

Bacardi South Beach Iced-Tea

3 oz. sweet-and-sour mix
½ oz. Bacardi light rum
½ oz. Bacardi Limón rum
½ oz. Bacardi spiced rum
Splash of cola

Combine the first four ingredients in a tall glass and add a splash of cola.

Bacardi Sparkling Cocktail

1 oz. Bacardi light rum
1 tsp. sugar
Dash bitters
Martini & Rossi Asti to fill

Mix the rum, sugar, and bitters in a tall glass. Fill with Asti.

Bacardi Tom & Jerry

1 egg
1 tsp. sugar
1 oz. Bacardi light or Gold rum
¼ oz. Bacardi Select rum
Boiling water
Grated nutmeg for garnish

Separate the yolk from white of egg and beat each separately. When white is fairly stiff, add sugar and beat to a stiff froth. Combine white and yolk. Put the Bacardi rums in mug, add boiling water, 1 tbsp. of egg mixture, and sprinkle with nutmeg.

Bacardi Top Gun

1 ¼ oz. Bacardi spiced rum
1 oz. orange juice
1 oz. pineapple juice
¼ oz. Bacardi 151 rum

Pour the Bacardi spiced rum into a glass filled with ice and add juices. Top with float of Bacardi 151 rum.

Bacardi Zombie

2 oz. Bacardi light rum
1 oz. Bacardi 151 rum (plus ¼ oz. to float, optional)
1 oz. Bacardi dark rum
1 oz. orange juice
1 oz. pineapple juice
Juice of 1 lemon or lime
Pineapple slice for garnish
Maraschino cherry for garnish
1 tsp. confectioners' sugar (optional)

Shake with ice and pour into tall glass. Garnish with pineapple slice and cherry. If desired, float ¼ oz. Bacardi 151 and 1 tsp. powdered sugar on top.

Bahama Mama

2 oz. orange juice
2 oz. pineapple juice
2 oz. sour mix
1 ½ oz. Whaler's Great White rum
1 ½ oz. Whaler's Rare Reserve Dark rum
1 ½ oz. Whaler's Vanillé rum
Ice cubes
Dash grenadine (optional)
Maraschino cherries for garnish
Orange slice for garnish

Shake first six ingredients well with ice. If using grenadine, add to the bottom of the serving glass before pouring. Pour into a chilled hurricane glass. Garnish with maraschino cherries, orange slice, and an umbrella.

Banana Colada

2 oz. Cruzan Banana rum
1 ½ oz. coconut milk
1 ½ oz. pineapple juice
Ice cubes

Blend until smooth.

Banana Mama

2 oz. pineapple juice
1 ½ oz. light rum
½ oz. dark rum
1 oz. banana liqueur
1 oz. Coco Lopez Cream of Coconut
1 oz. fresh or frozen strawberries

Blend.

Banana Man

1 oz. Bacardi light rum
½ oz. lemon juice or lime juice
¼ oz. banana liqueur
Ice cubes

Mix all ingredients in a blender and blend until smooth. Pour into a cocktail glass.

Barbados Cocktail

2 oz. Mount Gay rum
½ oz. Cointreau
½ oz. sweet-and-sour mix

Shake.

Bat Bite

1 lemon or lime wedge
Ice cubes
1 ¼ oz. Bacardi Select rum
¾ cup cranberry juice

Squeeze and drop a lime or lemon wedge into a
10-oz. glass filled with ice. Add the rum and juice.
Stir and serve.

Beachcomber

1 oz. Bacardi light or Gold rum
1 oz. lemon juice or lime juice
¼ oz. cherry liqueur
Ice cubes

Mix in a shaker or blender and strain into a
cocktail glass.

Beachcomber's Special

1 oz. Bacardi light rum
¾ oz. lemon juice or lime juice
¼ oz. orange curaçao
¼ tsp. sugar (optional)
Ice cubes

Mix in a shaker or blender and strain into a
cocktail glass or serve on the rocks.

Beach Party

1 ¼ oz. Bacardi light or Gold rum
1 oz. grenadine
1 oz. orange juice
1 oz. pineapple juice

Mix in a shaker or blender with ice and pour into a tall glass.

Bella Donna

Coarse sugar for rim
1 oz. Amaretto di Saronno
1 oz. Gosling's Black Seal rum
2 tbsp. fresh sour mix

Rim martini glass with sugar. Shake with ice. Strain into glass and serve.

 FROM THE LAS VEGAS BELLAGIO HOTEL

The Bermudan

2 oz. Gosling's Gold Bermuda rum
2 oz. pineapple juice
¼ oz. Grand Marnier
2 fresh mint leaves, torn
Lime twist for garnish

Shake vigorously and strain into a martini glass.
Garnish with twist of lime.

Between the Sheets

1 oz. fresh sweet-and-sour mix
½ oz. Cognac VSOP
½ oz. Pyrat XO Reserve rum
¼ oz. Citrónge liqueur
Coarse sugar for rim
Lemon twist for garnish

Shake and serve straight up in a glass with a
sugar-coated rim. Garnish with a lemon twist.

Bikini Daiquiri

2 oz. Coco Lopez Cream of Coconut
¾ oz. Cruzan Banana rum
¾ oz. Cruzan Pineapple rum
1 oz. lime juice
Crushed ice

Blend.

Black Maria

1 cup cold coffee
1 oz. Myers's dark rum
¾ oz. Tia Maria
1 tsp. sugar
Lemon peel for garnish

Stir. Garnish with a lemon peel.

Bolero Cocktail

¾ oz. Bacardi light or Gold rum
¼ oz. apple brandy
¼ oz. Martini & Rossi Rosso vermouth
Ice cubes
Lemon twist for garnish

Stir in a mixing glass with ice and strain into a chilled cocktail glass. Garnish with the lemon twist.

Bonbini

1 oz. Bacardi light or Gold rum
¼ oz. orange curaçao
Dash bitters
Ice cubes

Stir in a mixing glass with ice and strain into a chilled cocktail glass.

Brinley Coffee on the Rocks

3 oz. Brinley Gold Coffee rum
Crushed ice
Fresh coffee bean for garnish

Brinley Creamsicle

2 oz. Brinley Gold Vanilla rum
2 oz. orange juice
1 oz. milk
Ice cubes

Shake well and pour into a glass over ice.

Brinley Lime Fizz

4 parts club soda or lemon-lime soda
3 parts Brinley Gold Lime rum
Lime wedge for garnish

Pour into a tall glass over ice. Garnish with lime wedge.

Brinley "Spiked" Hot Chocolate

4 oz. hot chocolate
3 oz. Brinley Gold Vanilla rum
1 marshmallow for garnish
Chocolate shavings for garnish

Serve piping hot in a big mug. Top off with a marshmallow and chocolate shavings.

Café Con Chata

2 parts café con leche
1 part RumChata

Serve iced or hot.

California Lemonade

3 oz. lemon juice
1 ¼ oz. Bacardi light rum
1 ½ tsp. sugar
Dash bitters
Ice cubes
Club soda to fill

Pour the lemon juice, rum, sugar, and bitters into a tall glass half filled with ice. Fill with club soda and stir.

Calm Voyage

1 oz. Bacardi light or Gold rum
1 oz. orange juice
¼ oz. apple brandy
Dash orange bitters
Ice cubes

Mix in a shaker or blender and strain into a cocktail glass.

Cappuccino RumChata

2 oz. RumChata
Steaming hot coffee
Splash amaretto (optional)

Combine in a coffee mug. Add a splash of amaretto for more sweetness if desired.

Captain's Cruiser

3 oz. orange juice
2 oz. pineapple juice
1 ¼ oz. Captain Morgan Pirate Bay rum

Mix in a shaker. Pour into a tall glass over ice.

Captain's Pearl

½ ripe banana
1 ½ oz. half-and-half
1 oz. Captain Morgan Original Spiced Gold rum
¼ oz. amaretto
Scoop of crushed ice

Blend.

Caribbean Cocktail

1 ¼ oz. Bacardi light rum
1 oz. lemon juice or lime juice
1 oz. orange juice
Crushed or shaved ice
Club soda to fill
Orange slice for garnish
Red maraschino cherry for garnish

Pour the Bacardi rum and juices into a tall glass filled with crushed or shaved ice. Fill with soda and garnish with the fruit.

Caribbean Date

1 ½ oz. Pyrat XO Reserve rum
1 oz. tangerine purée
1 oz. Thai coconut milk
Ice cubes
Cinnamon for rim
Demerara sugar to rim glass
Mint sprig for garnish

Shake first three ingredients with ice and strain into a chilled cocktail glass rimmed with cinnamon and demerara sugar. Garnish with a fresh mint sprig.

Caribbean Joy

1 ¼ oz. Bacardi light rum
1 oz. pineapple juice
¾ oz. lemon juice
Ice cubes

Mix in shaker or blender and strain into a cocktail glass.

Cha-Ching (aka Take That to the Bank!)

3 parts RumChata
1 part Goldschlager

Serve over ice.

Champagne Tiki

1 oz. Cruzan Banana rum
1 oz. fresh strawberry coulis
1 oz. Pyrat XO Reserve rum
Juice ½ lime
Champagne to top
Fresh mint sprig for garnish
Sprinkle nutmeg for garnish

Shake first four ingredients and strain into 7 ½ oz. stem glass. Top with champagne. Garnish with a fresh mint sprig and sprinkle of nutmeg.

Cherried Cream Rum

1 ½ oz. White Rhum Barbancourt
½ oz. cherry brandy
½ oz. light cream

Shake.

Chicago Style

¾ oz. Bacardi light rum
½ oz. lemon juice or lime juice
¼ oz. anisette
¼ oz. triple sec
Ice cubes

Mix in a shaker or blender and strain into a cocktail glass.

Chocolate Cake

¾ oz. Whaler's Coconut rum
¾ oz. white crème de cacao
¼ oz. hazelnut liqueur
Splash half-and-half
Ice cubes
Whipped cream for garnish

Shake first four ingredients and strain into an old-fashioned glass over ice. Garnish with whipped cream.

Chocolate Cream

1 oz. heavy cream
¾ oz. Bacardi Gold rum
¼ oz. dark crème de cacao
¼ oz. white crème de menthe
Ice cubes

Mix in a shaker or blender and strain into a cocktail glass.

Cinnamon Toast Crunch Shooter

4 parts RumChata
1 part amaretto
Ice cubes
Cinnamon Toast Crunch cereal for garnish

Shake first two ingredients with ice and strain into a shot glass. Serve with a piece of Cinnamon Toast Crunch floating on top of shot.

Classic Daiquiri

1 ½ oz. Bacardi light rum
½ oz. lime juice or sweet-and-sour mix
½ tsp. sugar

Add the rum, lime juice, and sugar to a shaker with ice. Shake well and serve in a rocks glass.

. . .

Put a spin on the Classic Daiquiri with these variations.

Banana Daiquiri
Add one banana

Orange Daiquiri
Add 1 oz. orange juice

Peach Daiquiri
Add peeled, fresh peach half

Pineapple Daiquiri
Add ½ slice canned pineapple

Strawberry Daiquiri
Add 1 cup of strawberries

Substitute your favorite fruit or two or more fruits for your own special daiquiri.

Classic Hurricane

2 oz. Sailor Jerry Spiced Navy rum
1 tbsp. passion fruit syrup
2 tsp. lime juice
Ice cubes

Shake and strain into a cocktail glass.

Coco Lopez Limonade

3 oz. Coco Lopez Lemonade
1 oz. Bacardi Limón rum
Crushed ice

Blend.

Coco Lopez Limon Madness

1 oz. cranberry juice
1 oz. orange juice
½ oz. Bacardi Limón rum
½ oz. Coco Lopez Cream of Coconut
Crushed ice

Blend with crushed ice. Serve in a tall glass.

Coco Lopez Purple Passion

3 oz. Coco Lopez Purple Passion Colada Mix
1 ½ oz. Bacardi light rum
Crushed ice

Blend.

Cocomotion

1 ½ cups ice
4 oz. Coco Lopez Cream of Coconut
1 ½ oz. Puerto Rican dark rum
2 oz. lime juice

Blend.

Coco Naut

2 oz. Coco Lopez Cream of Coconut
2 oz. Wray & Nephew rum
¼ oz. fresh-squeezed lime juice
Crushed ice

Blend and serve in a tumbler.

Coconut Banana Colada

3 oz. pineapple juice
2 oz. Coco Lopez Cream of Coconut
2 oz. Cruzan Coconut rum
¾ oz. Cruzan Banana rum
Crushed ice

Blend.

Coconut Macaroon

1 part Kahlúa
1 part Malibu Original Caribbean rum
1 part RumChata
1 part heavy cream
Ice cubes

Shake with ice and pour into rocks glass.

Coconut Punch

2 oz. Coco Lopez Cream of Coconut
1 ¼ oz. Bacardi light or Gold rum
½ oz. lemon juice
3-4 tbsp. vanilla ice cream
Crushed ice

Mix all ingredients in a shaker or blender and pour into a tall glass.

Coffee Cream Cooler

1 ¼ oz. Bacardi light or Gold rum
Cold coffee to fill
Heavy cream to fill

Pour the rum into a tall glass half filled with ice. Fill with cold coffee and cream to desired proportions.

Combo Chata

1 part RumChata
1 part white crème de menthe
Ice cubes

Serve in a rocks glass over ice.

Cruzan Bay Breeze

1 part Cruzan Aged light rum
Ice cubes
Cranberry juice to top
Pineapple juice to top
Lime wedge for garnish

Build in an ice-filled highball glass. Top with cranberry juice and pineapple juice. Squeeze a lime wedge over and drop in.

Cruzan Cheesecake Martini

2 oz. Cruzan Vanilla rum
1 oz. cranberry juice
1 oz. pineapple juice

Shake with ice and strain into a martini glass.

Cruzan Gimlet

2 oz. Cruzan white rum
1 tbsp. sweetened lime juice
Ice cubes
Lemon or lime slice for garnish

Shake briskly and strain into a cocktail glass.
Garnish with lemon or lime slice.

Cruzan Island Mist

2 oz. Cruzan White or Gold rum
Crushed ice
Lemon twist for garnish

Pour rum into a small old-fashioned glass packed
with crushed ice. Garnish with the lemon twist.
Serve with short straws.

Cruzan Lemonade

2 parts Cruzan Aged Light rum
1 part lime juice
Ice cubes
Lemon-lime soda to fill
Lime wedge for garnish

Build in an ice-filled highball glass. Fill with lemon-lime soda. Squeeze a lime wedge over and drop in.

Cruzan Mai Tai

1 ½ oz. Cruzan Aged Light rum
½ oz. Cruzan Aged Dark rum
½ oz. curaçao
½ oz. lime juice
½ oz. orgeat syrup
1 tsp. superfine sugar
Cracked ice
Pineapple stick for garnish
Maraschino cherry for garnish

Pour all over cracked ice in an old-fashioned glass. Stir well. Garnish with pineapple stick and cherry. Serve with straw.

Cuba Libre

1 ¾ oz. Bacardi rum
Cola to taste
¼ lime

Pour the rum into glass and fill with cola to taste.
Add lime. Stir.

Dark 'n' Stormy

3 oz. ginger beer
1 ½ oz. Gosling's Black Seal rum
Lemon wedge to rim glass

Serve in a tall glass over ice. Squeeze a lemon
wedge around the rim of the glass. Garnish with
the lemon wedge.

The Derby Daiquiri
(Bermuda's National Drink)

1 ¼ oz. Bacardi light rum
½ oz. lemon juice or lime juice
½ oz. orange juice
Dash bitters
¼ tsp. sugar (optional)
Ice cubes

Mix in a shaker or blender and strain into a
cocktail glass.

Florida Sunrise

½ oz. grenadine
Crushed ice
1 ¼ oz. Bacardi light rum
Orange juice to fill

Pour the grenadine into the bottom of a tall glass. Fill with crushed ice. Pour in rum and fill with orange juice.

FrappuChata

2 parts iced coffee
1 part RumChata
Ice cubes

Combine in a blender. Blend until smooth. Serve in a tall glass.

Fuzzy Mango

3 oz. lemon-lime soda
2 oz. Brinley Gold Mango rum
Orange peel for garnish

Serve in a tall glass and garnish with orange peel.

Grasshopper

1 oz. Bacardi light rum
½ oz. cream
¼ oz. green crème de menthe
Crushed ice

Blend.

Havana Martini

1 ½ oz. Bacardi light-dry rum
½ oz. lime juice
½ tsp. sugar
Ice cubes
Lime twist for garnish

Combine first three ingredients in a shaker with ice and shake well. Strain into a chilled martini glass. Garnish with the lime twist.

Heat Wave

4 oz. orange juice
1 ¼ oz. Bacardi light or Gold rum
½ cup ice

Blend until smooth. Pour into a 10-oz. glass. Serve immediately.

In the Pink

1 ¼ oz. Myers's Original Rum cream
1 oz. Coco Lopez Cream of Coconut
1 tsp. grenadine
Ice cubes

Blend.

Kahlúa Colada

2 oz. pineapple juice
1 oz. Coco Lopez Cream of Coconut
1 oz. Kahlúa
½ oz. rum
1 cup ice

Blend.

Limón Cosmopolitan

2 oz. Bacardi Limón rum
1 oz. triple sec
½ oz. lime juice
Splash cranberry juice
Ice cubes
Lemon or orange twist for garnish

Shake the first four ingredients in a shaker with ice. Strain into a chilled martini glass and garnish with a lemon or orange twist.

The Limón Crantini

1 ½ oz. Bacardi Limón rum
¼ oz. Martini & Rossi extra dry vermouth
Cracked ice
Splash cranberry juice
Lemon twist for garnish

Add the rum and vermouth to a shaker with cracked ice. Add a splash of cranberry juice. Shake and strain into a martini glass. Garnish with the lemon twist.

Limón Drop

Superfine sugar
Lemon wedge
1 ½ oz. Bacardi Limón rum, chilled

Bite into a sugar-coated lemon wedge, but do not swallow. With the pulp still in your mouth, drink down the chilled Bacardi Limón.

Limón-on-the-Rocks

1 ¼ oz. Bacardi Limón rum
Lemon twist for garnish

Pour the Bacardi Limón over ice or crushed ice. Garnish with the lemon twist.

Mai Tai

½ oz. lime juice
½ oz. orange curaçao
½ oz. orgeat syrup
½ oz. simple syrup
Ice cubes
¾ oz. Bacardi light-dry rum
¼ oz. Bacardi 151 rum
Mint sprig for garnish
Pineapple spear for garnish
Red maraschino cherry for garnish.

Put the juice, orange curaçao, and syrups (or use Mai Tai mix) in an old-fashioned or stem glass half filled with cracked ice. Add the rums and stir gently. Garnish with the mint and fruits.

Malibu after Tan

1 part Malibu Caribbean Coconut rum
1 part white crème de cacao
2 scoops vanilla ice cream
Ice cubes

Blend and serve in a specialty glass.

Malibu Banana Split

1 part Malibu Caribbean Tropical Banana rum
Splash amaretto
Splash crème de cacao
Whipped cream for garnish
Maraschino cherry for garnish

Garnish with whipped cream and a cherry.

 DEVELOPED BY ORCHID LOUNGE, NYC

Malibu Blue Lagoon

4 parts pineapple juice
1 part Malibu Original Caribbean rum
¾ part blue curaçao

Mama Wana

1 oz. Cruzan Banana rum
1 oz. Cruzan Citrus rum
Ice cubes

Pour first two ingredients into a glass over chunky ice.

Mango Mambo

1 ½ oz. mango schnapps
1 ½ oz. Malibu Caribbean Tropical Banana rum
Ice cubes

Shake with ice. Strain into a chilled martini glass.

Mojito (Bee)

12 mint leaves
Crushed ice
Juice ½ lime
1 tbsp. honey
1 part Bacardi rum
3 parts club soda
Mint sprigs or lime wheel for garnish

Place mint leaves and crushed ice in a glass. Muddle well with a pestle. Add lime juice, honey, and Bacardi. Stir well. Top off with club soda. Stir and garnish with sprigs of mint or a lime wheel.

Mojito (Big Apple)

12 mint leaves
½ lime
½ part sugar
1 part Bacardi Big Apple rum
3 parts club soda
Mint sprigs for garnish
Lime wheel or green apple slice for garnish

Place mint leaves, lime, and sugar in a glass.
Crush well with a pestle. Add Bacardi Big Apple
Rum, top off with club soda, stir well, and garnish
with sprigs of mint and a lime wheel or green
apple slice.

Mojito (Coco Rum)

12 mint leaves
½ lime
1 part Bacardi Coconut rum
3 parts lemon-lime soda
Mint sprigs for garnish

Place mint leaves and lime in glass and crush
well. Add rum and soda, and garnish with sprigs
of mint.

Mojito (O)

12 mint leaves
½ lime
½ part sugar
1 part Bacardi O rum
3 parts club soda
Lime or orange wheel for garnish
Mint sprigs for garnish

Place mint leaves, lime, and sugar in a glass. Muddle well with a pestle. Add rum, top off with club soda, stir well, and garnish with a lime or orange wheel and sprigs of mint.

Mojito (Traditional/Cuban)

1 tbsp. lime juice
1 tbsp. sugar
6-inch mint sprig
1 oz. Bacardi light rum
Ice to fill
3 oz. club soda
2 dashes Angostura bitters

Place lime juice, sugar, and mint in a Collins glass. Crush mint stalk with pestle and muddle juice with sugar. Add rum, add ice to top of glass, and top off with club soda and bitters. Stir well.

Mount Gay Grinder

1 ½ oz. Mount Gay rum
Cranberry juice to fill
Splash lemon-lime soda

Serve in a tall glass.

Myers's Heat Wave

¾ oz. Myers's Original Dark rum
½ oz. peach schnapps
6 oz. pineapple juice
Splash grenadine

Pour first two ingredients into a glass over ice.
Fill with juice and top with grenadine.

Myers's Lounge Lizard

1 oz. Myers's Original Dark Rum
½ oz. Leroux amaretto
Ice cube
Cola to fill
Lime wedge for garnish

Mix first two ingredients in a tall glass over ice.
Fill with cola. Garnish with a lime wedge.

Ninetini

2 oz. sweet-and-sour mix
1 oz. Angostura 1919 Premium rum
½ oz. orange curaçao
½ tsp. sugar
4 dashes Angostura bitters

Shake.

Old San Juan Cocktail

1 ¼ oz. Bacardi Gold rum
½ oz. lemon juice or lime juice
¼ oz. grenadine
¼ oz. pineapple juice
Ice cubes

Stir in a mixing glass and strain into a cocktail glass.

Peach Banana Daiquiri

1 cup crushed ice
1 ½ oz. Puerto Rican light rum
1 oz. fresh lime juice
½ medium banana, diced
¼ cup sliced peaches

Blend.

Pink Panther

1 ¼ oz. Bacardi light rum
¾ oz. heavy cream
¾ oz. lemon juice
½ oz. grenadine
Ice cubes

Mix in a shaker or blender and strain into a cocktail glass.

Pirate's Punch

1 ¾ oz. Rhum Barbancourt 3 Star
¼ oz. sweet vermouth
Dash Angostura bitters

Shake.

Planter's Punch

2 tsp. superfine sugar
2 oz. orange juice
1 ¼ oz. Bacardi light rum
Splash Bacardi Gold rum
Cracked ice
Dash grenadine
Dark rum to float
Maraschino cherry for garnish
Orange slice for garnish

Place the sugar in a shaker or blender and dissolve with the orange juice. Add the rums, cracked ice, and mix well or blend until frothy. Strain into an 8-ounce glass with cracked ice. Float dark rum on top. Garnish with the cherry and orange slice.

Professor and Mary Anne

¾ part Malibu Caribbean Mango rum
½ part pineapple juice
¼ part Malibu Caribbean Banana rum

 DEVELOPED BY HAPPY ENDINGS, NEW YORK

Pyrat's Sin

1 sugar cube soaked with 2 dashes Angostura
    bitters
½ oz. Pyrat Cask 1623 rum
½ oz. Grand Marnier Cuvée de Cent
    Cinquantenaire liqueur
Chilled brut-style champagne to fill
Lemon peel for garnish
Strawberry slice for garnish

Place the sugar cube into a chilled champagne
glass. Add the rum and the Grand Marnier. Fill
with champagne. Garnish with lemon peel and
strawberry slice.

Racer's Edge

1 oz. Bacardi light rum
Ice cubes
Grapefruit juice to fill
¼ oz. green crème de menthe

Pour the rum into a tall glass half filled with
ice. Fill with grapefruit juice and float the green
crème de menthe on top.

Red Hot Mama

4 oz. cranberry juice
2 oz. club soda, chilled
1 ¼ oz. Bacardi light rum
Lime wedge for garnish

Serve in a 10-oz. glass and garnish with the lime wedge.

Root Beer Float

1 part RumChata
1 part root beer
Ice cubes

Combine first two ingredients over ice in a tall glass.

Rudolph's Nose

1 ½ oz. lemon juice
1 ¼ oz. Bacardi light or Gold rum
2 oz. cranberry juice
⅛ oz. grenadine

Mix in a tall glass. Add ice.

RumChata Chai Tea

3 parts room-temperature brewed tea
1 part RumChata
Ice cubes

Shake and pour into a tall glass.

Rum Milk Punch

4 oz. milk
1 ¾ oz. Rhum Barbancourt White
¾ oz. sugar cane syrup
Grated nutmeg for garnish

Blend first three ingredients and pour into a glass. Sprinkle with grated nutmeg.

Rum Runner

1 oz. Bacardi Select rum
1 oz. banana liqueur
1 oz. blackberry brandy
½ oz. Bacardi 151 rum
½ oz. grenadine
½ oz. lime juice
Ice cubes

Combine all ingredients in a blender and blend until frothy. Serve in a tall, stemmed glass.

Rum Russian

2 oz. Brinley Gold Coffee rum
1 oz. vodka
3 oz. milk

Serve in a tall glass.

Russian Seal

1 oz. Kahlúa
1 oz. Gosling's Black Seal rum
Ice cubes
Fresh milk to top

Shake first two ingredients and serve on the rocks. Top with fresh milk.

San Juan Cocktail

1 oz. Bacardi light rum
1 oz. grapefruit juice
½ oz. lemon or lime juice
¼ oz. Coco Lopez Cream of Coconut
¼ oz. Bacardi 151 rum

Mix the Bacardi light rum, juices, and cream of coconut in a shaker or blender with ice. Strain into a cocktail glass and float the 151 rum on top.

Scorpion

2 oz. orange juice
1 oz. light rum
½ oz. brandy
½ oz. gin
1 oz. sweet-and-sour mix
Dash bitters
Dash white crème de menthe
1 oz. white wine
Orchid for garnish

Blend first seven ingredients. Float the white wine. Garnish with an orchid.

Sex on the Boat

4 ½ oz. orange juice
1 oz. Captain Morgan Original Spiced Gold Rum
¼ oz. crème de banana
Scoop crushed ice

Blend.

Suffering Bastard

3 oz. orange juice
3 oz. sour mix
¼ oz. blue curaçao
¼ oz. gin
¼ oz. Sailor Jerry Spiced Navy rum
¼ oz. vodka
Dash cherry brandy
Ice cubes
Orange wheel for garnish

Pour into a hurricane glass over ice and stir.
Garnish with orange wheel.

Temptation

2 oz. cranberry juice
2 oz. Gosling's Gold Bermuda rum
¾ oz. triple sec
Ice cubes

Shake vigorously and strain into a martini glass.

Texas Sundowner

1 oz. Bacardi light rum
½ oz. grenadine
½ oz. Romana sambuca
Ice cubes

Pour first three ingredients into an old-fashioned glass with ice.

Tropical Breeze

4 oz. cranberry juice
1 ¼ oz. Captain Morgan Original Spiced Gold rum
Mint sprig for garnish

Serve on the rocks. Garnish with mint sprig.

Tropical Storm

1 oz. Bacardi light rum
Grapefruit juice to fill
¼ oz. blackberry brandy

Pour the rum into a tall glass half filled with ice. Fill with grapefruit juice and float the blackberry brandy on top.

Vampire

2 oz. Cruzan Vanilla rum
Ice cubes
2 oz. lemon-lime soda
Splash grenadine

Pour Cruzan Vanilla Rum into a highball glass over ice. Fill with lemon-lime soda and top with grenadine.

Wave Cutter

1 ½ oz. Mount Gay rum
1 oz. cranberry juice
1 oz. orange juice

Shake.

Yellow Bird

2 oz. orange juice
2 oz. pineapple juice
¾ oz. Don Q Limón rum
¼ oz. crème de banana
¼ oz. Galliano
Ice cubes
Maraschino cherry for garnish
Orange slice for garnish
Pineapple ring for garnish

Shake the first five ingredients well with ice. Pour into a tall glass with ice cubes. Garnish with the cherry, orange slice, and pineapple ring.

Zaya Abilene

3 oz. orange juice
2 oz. peach nectar
1 ½ oz. Zaya Rum
Ice cubes

Pour first three ingredients into a highball glass filled with ice cubes. Stir well and enjoy.

Zaya Black Velvet

10 oz. lager
1 oz. Zaya Rum

Pour into a beer mug or large glass and enjoy.

Zaya Gauguin

1 ¼ oz. Zaya Rum
½ oz. lemon juice
½ oz. lime juice
½ oz. passion fruit syrup
Ice cubes

Combine first four ingredients in a shaker with ice. Strain into martini glass.

Zaya Shark Tooth

½ oz. Zaya Rum
¼ oz. grenadine
¼ oz. lemon juice
¼ oz. lime juice
Splash soda water

Pour rum, grenadine, lemon juice, and lime juice into a Collins glass. Stir, and add a splash of soda water.

Zaya Sweetie

3 oz. apple juice
¾ oz. Zaya Rum
½ oz. amaretto almond liqueur
Crushed ice

Blend, pour into cocktail glass, and enjoy.

Zaya Tart

2 oz. Zaya Rum
Ice cubes
4 oz. pomegranate juice

Pour Zaya Rum into glass filled with ice. Fill with pomegranate juice and stir.

Zaya Yacht Club

2 oz. Zaya Rum
1 oz. Grand Marnier
Ice cubes
Lime twist for garnish

Combine first two ingredients over ice in a double old-fashioned glass. Garnish with the lemon twist.

Zombie

¾ oz. Bacardi Limón rum
¼ oz. Limón Gold rum
1 oz. lemon juice or lime juice
1 oz. orange juice
1 oz. pineapple juice
Ice cubes
¼ oz. Limón 151 rum (optional)
1 tsp. superfine sugar (optional)
Pineapple spear for garnish
Red maraschino cherry for garnish

Mix the first two rums and juices with ice in a shaker or blender and pour into a tall glass. If desired, float ¼ tsp. Bacardi 151 rum on top with 1 tsp. superfine sugar. Garnish with the pineapple and cherry.

Cachaca Rum Recipes

Cachaca is a liquor made from fermented sugarcane. It is the most popular distilled beverage in Brazil. The major difference between cachaca and rum is that rum is usually made from molasses, a by-product from refineries that boil the cane juice to extract as much sugar crystal as possible, while cachaca is made from fresh sugarcane juice that is fermented and distilled.

Brazilian Pain Killa'

1 ½ oz. Leblon Cachaca
1 ½ oz. pineapple juice
¾ oz. fresh clementine/tangerine juice
½ oz. double-coconut falernum
2 dashes Angostura orange bitters
Ice cubes
Orange slice for garnish
Pink flamingo for garnish
Grated cinnamon for garnish
Grated nutmeg for garnish

Dry shake first five ingredients and pour over fresh ice. Garnish with an orange slice and pink flamingo. Grate cinnamon and nutmeg on top.

Brazilian Presidente

2 oz. Leblon Cachaca
½ oz. fig liqueur
½ oz. sweet vermouth
Dash grenadine
Ice cubes
Fig for garnish

Shake first four ingredients on ice. Strain and serve up in a chilled martini glass. Garnish with a fig.

Caipirinha

1 lime
Sugar to taste
2 oz. cachaca
Ice cubes

Wash the lime and roll it on the board to loosen the juices. Cut the lime into pieces and place them in a glass. Sprinkle with the sugar and crush the pieces (pulp side up) with a pestle. Add the cachaca and stir to mix. Add the ice and stir again.

Candy Cane Caipirinha

2 tsp. sugar
½ lime cut into eighths
Ice
2 oz. Leblon Cachaca
Splash peppermint schnapps
Candy cane stick for garnish

Muddle the sugar and lime pieces in a shaker.
Add ice and Leblon Cachaca. Shake thoroughly.
Pour the shaker contents into a rocks glass and
float the schnapps on top. Garnish with a peppermint candy cane stick.

Leblon James

3 oz. watermelon
1 ½ oz. chipotle-infused agave nectar
1 ½ oz. Leblon Cachaca
¼ lime
¼ orange
Ice cubes
2 basil leaves for garnish
Orange twist for garnish

Puree watermelon with agave nectar. Combine
with the cachaca, lime, and orange in a mixing
tumbler. Add ice and shake vigorously. Strain
into a martini glass. Garnish with basil leaves
and an orange twist.

Leblon-Lychee Popsicle

4 oz. coconut water
1 ½ oz. Leblon Cachaca
1 oz. Boiron Lychee Puree
1 oz. simple syrup
¾ oz. fresh lemon juice
Pinch coconut shavings

Mix all ingredients in a mixing glass. Pour into your favorite Popsicle mold. Put in freezer and freeze until solid.

Mai Kind of Tai

10 chunks fresh pineapple, plus extra for garnish
Ice cubes
8 oz. Leblon Cachaca
4 oz. orange juice
4 oz. pineapple juice
2 oz. triple sec
Splash grenadine

Muddle fresh pineapple in a carafe. Add ice, Leblon, orange juice, pineapple juice, triple sec, and grenadine. Stir very well. Pour into a Leblon Carafe and serve on the rocks. Garnish with some fresh pineapples inside the glass.

Strawberry Bellini

2 lemon wedges
2 strawberries cut into fourths
½ oz. simple syrup
Ice
2 oz. Leblon Cachaca
1 oz. champagne
¼ oz. raspberry liqueur

Muddle the lemon wedges, strawberries, and simple syrup in a shaker. Fill shaker with ice and add Leblon Cachaca. Shake vigorously, then strain into a flute. Add champagne and top with raspberry liqueur.

SCOTCH

Aberdeen Sour

1 ½ oz. Cutty Sark
1 oz. lemon juice
1 oz. orange juice
½ oz. triple sec
1 scoop crushed ice

Shake or blend. Pour into an old-fashioned glass.

Affinity

1 oz. Cutty Sark
½ oz. Martini & Rossi extra dry vermouth
½ oz. Martini & Rossi Rosso sweet vermouth
2 dashes orange bitters
Ice cubes

Stir well. Strain into a cocktail glass.

The BBtini

2 oz. Black Bottle Scotch whiskey
½ oz. St. Germain Elderflower liqueur
Splash grenadine
Splash simple syrup
Ice cubes
3 raspberries for garnish

Shake first four ingredients with ice. Strain and serve in a chilled martini glass. Garnish with 3 raspberries.

Black Italian

1 oz. red Italian vermouth
1 oz. Black Bottle Scotch whiskey
2 drops vanilla concentrate
Maraschino cherry for garnish

Serve in an old-fashioned glass over ice. Garnish with a cherry.

Black Jack

1 oz. Cutty Sark
½ oz. triple sec
½ oz. Kahlúa
½ oz. lemon juice
Ice cubes

Combine first four ingredients in a shaker half-filled with ice. Shake well. Strain into a cocktail glass.

Black Lady

2 oz. Black Bottle Scotch whiskey
⅓ oz. crème de cacao
½ oz. lemon juice
1 oz. plum
1 oz. strawberry
1 oz. ginger puree
1 tsp. cocoa powder

Shake. Serve over ice.

Blimey

1 ½ oz. Cutty Sark Scotch whiskey
½ oz. lime juice
1 ½ tsp. superfine sugar
Ice cubes

Combine first three ingredients in a shaker half-filled with ice. Shake well. Strain into a cocktail glass.

Bobby Burns

1 oz. scotch
¼ oz. Martini & Rossi sweet vermouth
3 dashes Benedictine
Ice cubes

Stir and serve.

Colonel MacDonald, or Whiskey Mac

1 ½ oz. Black Bottle Scotch whiskey
1 ½ oz. Stone's Original Green Ginger wine
Ice cubes

Serve over ice.

Cutty Caribbean

1 ½ oz. Cutty Sark
½ oz. blue curaçao
½ oz. Coco Lopez Real Cream of Coconut
Ice cubes
Lemon slice for garnish

Shake first three ingredients well with ice. Strain into a cocktail glass and serve with two straws. Garnish with the lemon slice.

Cutty Clipper

1 ½ oz. Cutty Sark
½ oz. crème de cacao
½ oz. heavy cream
Ice cubes
Dash grenadine
Orange slice for garnish

Add first three ingredients to ice in a shaker
and shake well. Strain into a cocktail glass and
add a dash of grenadine. Serve with two straws.
Garnish with the orange slice.

Cutty Crows Nest

1 measure Cutty Sark
1 measure Stone's Original Green Ginger wine
1 measure Tia Maria
Ice cubes
Heavy cream for float
Grated chocolate for garnish

Add first three ingredients to ice in a shaker.
Shake well, strain into a cocktail glass. Float
cream on top and garnish with grated chocolate.

Cutty Mizzen

1 measure Cutty Sark
1 measure Martini & Rossi dry vermouth
1 measure Midori Melon liqueur
Dash blue curaçao
Ice cubes

Stir in a shaker glass. Pour into a cocktail glass.

Cutty Square Rigger

1 measure Cutty Sark
1 measure Martini & Rossi extra dry vermouth
Dash lime juice
Ice cubes
Ginger ale to fill

Add first three ingredients to ice in a shaker. Stir
and pour into a glass. Top with ginger ale.

Cutty Surfer

1 measure Cutty Sark
½ measure blue curaçao
½ measure orange curaçao
Ice cubes
Club soda to fill
Orange slice for garnish
Green maraschino cherry for garnish

Shake the first three ingredients well with ice, and top with club soda. Garnish with the orange slice and cherry.

Donnie's Dram

2 oz. Black Bottle Scotch whiskey
Muddled mint leaves
Ice cubes
Ginger ale

Combine first three ingredients in a rocks glass. Top with ginger ale.

Flying Scotsman

3 measures Cutty Sark
2 ½ measures Martini & Rossi vermouth
1 tbsp. Angostura bitters
1 tbsp. sugar syrup
Ice cubes

Shake first four ingredients and serve in a rocks glass over ice.

Gale Warning

3 oz. pineapple juice
2 oz. cranberry juice
1 oz. Cutty Sark
Ice cubes

Serve over ice in a tall glass.

Glasgow

2 oz. Black Bottle Scotch whiskey
1 oz. French vermouth
1 tsp. absinthe
Dash Angostura bitters
Ice cubes

Shake well and strain into a cocktail glass.

Godfather

2 parts amaretto
2 parts Cutty Sark
Ice cubes

Stir on the rocks.

Heather Berry

3 oz. apple juice
2 oz. Black Bottle Irish whiskey
1 oz. blueberry liqueur
20 red currants

Shake. Serve over ice in a tall glass.

Heather Coffee

Coffee to fill
1 oz. Cutty Sark
¼ oz. Drambuie liqueur
Whipped cream for garnish

Fill a mug with coffee and add the Cutty Sark
and Drambuie. Garnish with the whipped cream.

Herman's Pride

1 ½ oz. Pinch Blended Scotch whiskey
1 ½ oz. sweetened lemon mix
½ oz. Cointreau

Shake well and serve on the rocks.

Islay Punch

2 ½ oz. Black Bottle Scotch whiskey
2 oz. water
¼ oz. lime juice
½ oz. simple syrup
2 dashes Angostura bitters
Ice cubes

Serve over ice.

John Collins

3 oz. sweetened lemon mix
1 ½ oz. Pinch Blended Scotch whiskey
Club soda to fill
Maraschino cherry for garnish
Orange slice for garnish

Shake with ice, and pour into a tall glass with ice.
Fill with club soda. Add cherry and orange slice.

Mamie Taylor

1 ¼ oz. Cutty Sark
¼ oz. fresh lime juice
Ice cubes
Ginger ale to fill

Build in a tall glass with ice. Top with ginger ale.

Perfect Rob Roy

1 ¼ oz. Cutty Sark
¼ oz. Martini & Rossi extra dry vermouth
¼ oz. Martini & Rossi Rosso sweet vermouth
Ice cubes
Lemon twist for garnish

Serve in a rocks glass with ice with the lemon twist for garnish.

Presbyterian

2 oz. Black Bottle Scotch whiskey
2-4 oz. ginger ale
Ice cubes

Serve over ice in a tall glass.

P.S.

1 ½ oz. Pinch Blended Scotch whiskey
¾ oz. peppermint schnapps
Dash Cointreau
Ice cubes

Stir on the rocks.

Purple Heather

1 measure Cutty Sark
1 tsp. crème de cassis
Club soda to fill

Pour the Cutty Sark and crème de cassis into a
tall glass and top up with club soda.

Real McCoy

Cutty Sark
Water or club soda to taste

Serve in a tall glass.

Rob Roy

Equal measures:
Cutty Sark
Martini & Rossi Italian vermouth
Ice cubes
Dash Angostura bitters

Shake first three ingredients with ice and strain into a chilled cocktail glass. Stir in the bitters.

Rusty Nail

1 ½ oz. Cutty Sark
½ oz. Drambuie liqueur
Ice cubes

Serve on the rocks.

Rusty Screw

1 ¾ oz. Black Bottle Scotch whiskey
¾ oz. Drambuie liqueur
⅛ oz. Solemo Blood Orange liqueur
Orange slice for garnish

Combine all ingredients in a Boston glass. Shake and double strain into an old-fashioned glass. Garnish with an orange slice.

Scarlet Schooner

2 oz. cranberry juice
2 oz. Cutty Sark
1 oz. peach schnapps

Stir in a tall glass with ice.

Scotch and Lime

2 ½ oz. Black Bottle Scotch whiskey
¼ oz. lime juice
Ice cubes

Serve over ice.

Scotch Horse's Neck

1 measure Cutty Sark
5-6 dashes lemon juice
1 dash Angostura bitters
Ginger ale to fill

Pour first three ingredients into a large glass and add ginger ale.

Scotch Old-Fashioned

½ tsp. sugar
2 dashes Angostura bitters
Lemon twist
Maraschino cherry
Orange slice
2 oz. Cutty Sark
Ice cubes
Splash club soda

Muddle sugar, bitters, lemon twist, cherry, and orange slice in an old-fashioned glass. Add the Cutty Sark and ice and top with club soda.

Scotch Revenge

2 oz. Black Bottle Scotch whiskey
½ oz. Georgia Moon Corn whiskey
1 brown sugar cube
Dash Angostura bitters

Shake. Serve over ice.

Scotch Rickey

1 measure Cutty Sark
Juice ½ lime
Juice ¼ lemon
Club soda to fill
1 ice cube

Stir first four ingredients. Pour into a tall glass with ice.

Scotch Toddy

Heaping teaspoonful sugar
3 oz. boiling water
1 ½ oz. Cutty Sark

Put a heaping teaspoon of sugar in a warm glass; add a little boiling water to dissolve the sugar. Add 1 oz. of Cutty Sark and stir. Pour in more boiling water and top with remaining Cutty Sark.

Scotty Dog

1 ½ oz. lime juice
1 ¼ oz. Cutty Sark
Lime slice for garnish

Shake. Garnish with a slice of lime.

Sherried Scotch

1 part Pinch Blended Scotch whiskey
1 part Duff Gordon sherry
Ice cubes

Stir well with ice.

Skinny Scotch

2 oz. Pinch Blended Scotch whiskey
Ice cubes
Diet soda to fill
Lemon twist for garnish

Put whiskey into a tall glass filled with ice. Fill with your favorite diet soda. Add twist of lemon.

Smokey Martini

3 oz. Black Bottle Scotch whiskey
1 ½ oz. gin or vodka

Shake and strain into a chilled martini glass.

Taste of Honey

2 oz. Cutty Sark
1 oz. heavy cream
½ oz. honey
Ice cubes

Blend. Serve in a cocktail glass.

Whisper

2 oz. Cutty Sark
½ oz. Martini & Rossi dry vermouth
½ oz. Martini & Rossi sweet vermouth
Cracked ice

Serve over cracked ice.

Wicked Sky

2 oz. Black Bottle Scotch whiskey
1 ½ oz. Midori Melon liqueur
Dash Angostura bitters
Pineapple juice to fill

In a shaker with ice add Black Bottle and Midori. Shake well and pour over ice into a highball glass. Add bitters and fill with pineapple juice.

Wood-Ward

1 oz. Cutty Sark
1 oz. grapefruit juice
1 oz. Martini & Rossi extra dry vermouth
Ice cubes

Combine first three ingredients with ice; shake well. Strain into an old-fashioned glass with ice.

1800 Bloody Maria

Ice cubes
1 ½ oz. 1800 tequila
6 oz. Bloody Mary mix
Chilled lime wedge for garnish

Place ice cubes in a large wine glass and add tequila. Fill glass with Bloody Mary mix. Stir. Garnish with the lime wedge.

1800 Celebration

½ oz. 1800 tequila
Champagne to fill

Pour the tequila into a glass and add champagne.

1800 Lemon Drop

1 ¼ oz. 1800 tequila
1 oz. lemon-lime soda
1 oz. sweet-and-sour mix
½ oz. triple sec
Ice cubes
Squeeze fresh lemon
Lemon wheel for garnish

Pour first four ingredients over ice in a rocks glass. Mix. Float fresh lemon juice. Garnish with lemon wheel.

1800 Sunset

3 oz. champagne
1 oz. 1800 tequila
Splash grenadine

Acapulco

2 oz. pineapple juice
2 oz. tequila
Lemon-lime soda
Ice cubes

Pour first two ingredients into a glass and fill with lemon-lime soda. Serve in an old-fashioned glass with ice.

Acapulco Clam Digger

3 oz. clam juice
3 oz. tomato juice
2 oz. tequila
½ tsp. horseradish
Several dashes Tabasco sauce
Several dashes Worcestershire sauce
Cracked ice
Dash lemon juice

Mix first six ingredients thoroughly with cracked ice in a double old-fashioned glass. Top with lemon juice.

Agavero Sunset

2 oz. Agavero Tequila liqueur
1 large scoop vanilla ice cream

Float tequila over the top of the ice cream. Enjoy with a 1 oz. side shot of Agavero, if desired.

Arriba

3 oz. orange juice
1 ½ oz. 1800 tequila
Ice cubes
¼ oz. Grand Marnier

Mix orange juice and tequila in a tall glass with ice. Float Grand Marnier on top.

Avocado Margarita

1 ½ oz. silver tequila
1 oz. half-and-half
1 oz. lime juice
½ oz. Cointreau
½ oz. lemon juice
¼ cup diced ripe avocado
1 tsp. sugar
Ice cubes
Lime slice for garnish
Avocado slice for garnish

Combine first seven ingredients in a blender with ice and blend until smooth. Pour into a chilled cocktail glass. Garnish with a lime slice and avocado slice.

Aztec Ruin

1 part lime juice
1 part Jose Cuervo Tradicional tequila

Serve either as a chilled shot or in a martini glass.

Banana Boat

1 ½ oz. Tarantula Reposado tequila
1 oz. lime juice
½ oz. banana liqueur

Serve over ice or as a shot.

Bee Sting

2 oz. fresh-squeezed blood orange juice
1 ½ oz. Patrón Reposado tequila
½ oz. Marie Brizard Crème de Cassis
½ oz. clover honey syrup
Juice 1 lime, hand extracted
Ice cubes
Blackberries for garnish
Raspberries for garnish

Shake first five ingredients with ice until well-blended. Strain into a 14-oz. goblet over ice. Garnish with blackberries and raspberries.

Berry Medley

1 ½ oz. Patrón Silver tequila
1 oz. fresh sweet-and-sour
1 oz. pineapple juice
¾ oz. Chambord
3 fresh raspberries (plus 1 for garnish)
Ice cubes
Peach schnapps to float
Pineapple spear

Shake first five ingredients with ice. Strain and serve over ice. Float the schnapps, and garnish with a pineapple spear with a fresh raspberry on top.

Billionaire's Margarita

5 oz. crushed ice
2 oz. freshly squeezed lime juice
1 ½ oz. Jose Cuervo Reserva de la Familia
    tequila
½ oz. Grand Marnier Cuvée de Cent
    Cinquantenaire liqueur
Lime wedge for garnish

Shake well and strain into a glass with ice.
Garnish with a lime wedge.

Black Cat

1 part amaretto
1 part Jose Cuervo tequila

Serve as a shot.

Black Turncoat

1 ½ oz. Jose Cuervo Black Medallion tequila
Ice cubes
Juice ½ lime
Splash mineral water
Cola

Pour tequila into a glass over ice. Add the juice
of ½ lime and a splash of mineral water. Fill to
taste with cola. Stir.

Bloody Hurricane

2 oz. tequila
Ice cubes
1 can lemon-lime soda
½ oz. grenadine

Pour tequila over ice into a highball glass. Add lemon-lime soda to the top and add grenadine. Allow to chill for a few seconds.

Bloody Maria

3 oz. tomato juice
2 oz. tequila
Dash celery salt
Dash lemon juice
Dash pepper
Dash salt
Dash Tabasco sauce
Cracked ice
Lime slice or celery stick for garnish

Shake with cracked ice and strain into a Collins glass over ice cubes. Garnish with a slice of lime or celery stick.

Blue Agave

1 oz. blue curaçao
1 oz. Jose Cuervo Tradicional tequila
Ice cubes

Shake, strain, and serve.

Blue Moon-A-Rita

1 ½ oz. lime juice
1 ½ oz. Jose Cuervo Platino tequila
½ oz. blue curaçao
½ oz. Cointreau
Ice cubes

Serve on the rocks.

Blue Smoke

1 ¼ oz. Jose Cuervo tequila
3 oz. orange juice
Crushed ice
½ oz. blue curaçao

Pour tequila and orange juice into a chilled wine glass with finely crushed ice. Stir. Float blue curaçao on top.

Bomshel

1 oz. Tequila Rose
1 oz. McCormick vodka

Serve as a shot.

Bon Voyage

1 oz. gin
1 oz. Jose Cuervo tequila
Ice cubes
Dash lemon juice
Dash blue curaçao

Pour the first two ingredients over ice into a cocktail glass. Mix in a dash of lemon juice and a dash of blue curaçao. Stir lightly. Best when drunk with a straw.

Brave Bull

2 oz. tequila
½ oz. coffee liqueur
Ice cubes

Pour tequila and coffee liqueur over ice cubes in a rocks glass. Stir.

Cabo

3 oz. pineapple juice
1 ½ oz. Jose Cuervo tequila
¼ oz. lime juice
Ice cubes

Shake first three ingredients well in a shaker half-filled with ice cubes. Strain into a cocktail glass.

Camper

2 oz. orange juice
2 oz. pineapple juice
1 ½ oz. tequila
Ice cubes
½ oz. Chambord

Pour the first three ingredients into a highball glass almost filled with ice cubes. Stir well. Drop the Chambord into the center of the drink.

Checkers

1 can beer
1 oz. tequila

Pour the beer in a mug, drop in the shot of tequila, stir, and drink.

Cherry Bomb

2 oz. maraschino cherry juice
1 ½ oz. Jose Cuervo Tradicional tequila
½ oz. cherry liqueur
Ice cubes

Shake, strain, and serve.

Chihuaha

2 oz. tequila
Grapefruit juice to fill
Salt to rim glass

Pour tequila into a glass and fill with grapefruit juice. Salt rim of highball glass then add sip stick.

Chocolate Cream Soda

1 ½ oz. Tequila Rose Cocoa
½ oz. half-and-half
Ice cubes
Soda to fill
Maraschino cherry for garnish

Build first two ingredients in a highball glass with ice and fill with soda. Garnish with speared cherry.

Chocolate Strawberry

1 oz. Tequila Rose
½ oz. milk
½ oz. chocolate liqueur
Hot coffee to fill
Whipped cream to top

Fill with hot coffee and top with whipped cream.

Cinco de Mayo

2 ½ oz. tequila
1 oz. grenadine
1 oz. Rose's Lime Juice
Ice cubes
Lime wedge for garnish

Mix first three ingredients well with ice and strain into a chilled cocktail glass. Garnish with a lime wedge.

Cinco de Mayo #2

1 ¾ oz. cranberry juice
1 ½ oz. El Mayor Blanco tequila
¾ oz. Juarez triple sec
Ice cubes
Lime wedge for garnish

Shake first three ingredients well with ice and strain into a chilled martini glass. Garnish with a lime wedge.

The Clasico Shot

2 oz. Jose Cuervo Tradicional tequila
Pinch salt
Lime wedge

Pour tequila into a shot glass. Lick skin between thumb and forefinger. Sprinkle salt on moist skin. Drink shot all at once and quickly. Lick salt and suck lime wedge.

Confetti Drops

1 oz. Jose Cuervo Especial Gold tequila
½ oz. Goldschlager

Serve chilled in a shot glass.

Corralejo Cactus

2 oz. Irish Cream liqueur
1 oz. Tequila Corralejo

Pour ingredients into an old-fashioned glass. Stir and serve.

Corralejo Turbo

1 oz. pineapple juice
1 oz. Tequila Corralejo
1 oz. vodka
Crushed ice

Pour ingredients into a cocktail shaker. Shake well. Pour into a tall glass. Serve immediately.

Country Rose

3 oz. milk
1 oz. Tequila Rose
½ oz. amaretto
½ oz. Southern Comfort bourbon
½ oz. strawberry schnapps
Ice cubes

Mix first five ingredients and pour over ice.

Cuervo Acapulco Fizz

2 oz. orange juice
1 ½ oz. cream
1 ½ oz. Jose Cuervo Especial Gold tequila
1 whole egg
2 tsp. granulated sugar
2 dashes orange bitters
3 ice cubes
Orange slice for garnish

Blend all ingredients together. Pour into a high-ball glass and garnish with the orange slice.

Cuervo Agua Fresca

Agua Fresca mixture:
1 cup water
⅓ cup cubed fresh pineapple
⅓ cup fresh or frozen whole strawberries
⅓ cup fresh or frozen cubed ripe mango
½ cup ice (3 oz.)
2 tbsp. superfine sugar
1 tbsp. fresh lime juice
2 sprigs fresh mint

4 cups ice, divided
12 oz. Jose Cuervo Gold tequila, divided
Strawberries for garnish

Combine all Agua Fresca ingredients in a blender. Blend until smooth. Strain into a pitcher. Chill. For each serving: in a 13-oz. hurricane glass, place about ½ cup ice. Add 1 ½ oz. Cuervo Gold. Fill glass with about 5 oz. Agua Fresca mixture. Garnish with strawberries.

Makes about 8 servings.

Cuervo Baja Gold

1 ½ oz. Jose Cuervo Gold tequila
1 oz. sugar syrup
½ oz. fresh lime juice
2–3 oz. ice cold beer
Lime slice for garnish

Mix first three ingredients in blender with crushed ice. Pour into a chilled mug. Add beer. Garnish with a lime slice.

Cuervo Brave Bull

1 ½ oz. coffee liqueur
1 ½ oz. Cuervo Tradicional
Ice cubes
Lemon twist for garnish

Combine first two ingredients in a rocks glass with ice. Garnish with the lemon twist.

Cuervo Cactus Cooler

1 ½ oz. Jose Cuervo Especial Gold tequila
Club soda to fill
Ice cubes
½ oz. peppermint schnapps
Lime wheel for garnish

Pour tequila and club soda over rocks in a tall glass. Top with peppermint schnapps and garnish with the lime wheel.

Cuervo Crandaddy

5 oz. cranberry juice
1 oz. Jose Cuervo Especial Gold tequila
1 oz. triple sec
Ice cubes

Pour first three ingredients into a large glass with ice. Stir.

Cuervo Golden Breeze

1 ½ oz. Jose Cuervo Especial Gold tequila
Ice cubes
4 oz. grapefruit juice
2 oz. cranberry juice
Squeeze fresh lime
Lime wedge for garnish

Pour the Cuervo Gold over ice in a 12 or 13-oz. glass. Add juices and stir. Garnish with the lime wedge.

Cuervo Gold Margarita

2 oz. lime juice
2 oz. sweet-and-sour mix
1 ½ oz. Jose Cuervo Especial Gold
1 oz. triple sec
Ice cubes

Blend ingredients and pour into a margarita glass over ice or frozen.

Cuervo Lolita

1 ½ oz. Jose Cuervo Especial Gold tequila
1 tsp. honey
Juice 1 lime
Dash bitters

Combine all ingredients in a cocktail shaker with ice. Strain into a cocktail glass.

Cuervo Mexican Coffee

6 oz. fresh hot coffee
1 oz. 1800 tequila
¾ oz. Kahlúa
Whipped cream for garnish

Add the tequila and Kahlúa to a mug of coffee. Garnish with whipped cream.

Cuervo Orange Margarita

3 oz. orange juice
1 ½ oz. Jose Cuervo Especial Gold tequila
½ oz. triple sec
½ oz. sweet-and-sour mix
Strawberries for garnish

Blend. Garnish with strawberries.

Cuervo Piñata

5 oz. pineapple juice
1 ½ oz. Jose Cuervo Especial Gold tequila
Ice cubes
Fresh pineapple spear for garnish

Pour the juice and tequila into a tall glass with
ice. Garnish with a pineapple spear.

Cuervo Raspberry Margarita

½ cup frozen raspberries
1 ½ oz. Jose Cuervo Especial Gold tequila
1 oz. lime juice
1 oz. triple sec
½ cup ice
Fresh raspberries for garnish

Combine first four ingredients in a blender with
ice. Blend until frothy. Garnish with raspberries.

Cuervo Santa Fe Maggie

2 oz. cranberry juice
2 oz. sweet-and-sour mix
1 ¼ oz. Jose Cuervo Especial Gold tequila
½ oz. triple sec
Lime wedge for garnish

Blend ingredients briefly with ice and pour into
an unsalted margarita glass. Squeeze in a lime
wedge and drop into the glass.

Cuervo Side Out

2 oz. cranberry juice
1 ½ oz. Cuervo Gold
1 ½ oz. lime juice
1 oz. triple sec
Crushed ice
Lime wheel for garnish

Blend first five ingredients and strain into a large
margarita glass. Garnish with the lime wheel.

Cuervo Slammer

1 oz. lemon-lime soda, chilled
½ oz. Jose Cuervo Especial Gold tequila

Serve as a shot.

Cuervo Spike

1 ½ oz. Jose Cuervo Especial Gold tequila
Ice cubes
Grapefruit juice to fill

Pour tequila over ice in a tall glass, add grapefruit juice, and stir.

Cuervo Sunburn

1 ½ oz. cranberry juice cocktail
1 ½ oz. freshly squeezed orange juice
1 ½ oz. pineapple juice
1 ½ oz. Jose Cuervo Especial Gold tequila
1 cup ice
Maraschino cherry for garnish
Orange wedge for garnish

Shake all drink ingredients with ½ cup ice. Place ½ cup of ice in a 13-oz. balloon glass. Strain drink over ice and garnish with the cherry and orange wedge.

Cuervo Sunrise

4 oz. freshly squeezed orange juice
1 ½ oz. Jose Cuervo Especial Gold tequila
Ice cubes
¼ oz. grenadine

Pour the orange juice and tequila in a tall glass with ice. Slowly pour in grenadine.

Death at Night

½ shot tequila
½ shot black sambuca

Layer in a shot glass and serve.

Double Gold Medals

½ oz. Jose Cuervo Especial Gold tequila
½ oz. Goldwasser

Combine ingredients in a shot glass.

Durango Drop

1 ½ oz. Jose Cuervo Especial Gold tequila
½ oz. lemon juice
Coarse sugar for rim

Serve in a sugar-rimmed shot glass.

El Diablo

1 oz. lime juice
1 oz. Tequila Corralejo
½ oz. crème de cassis
½ cup ginger ale
Lime wedge for garnish

Mix ingredients in a tall glass. Top with ginger ale and garnish with a lime wedge.

El Dorado

2 oz. Patrón tequila
1 ½ oz. lemon juice
1 tbsp. honey
Ice cubes
Orange slice for garnish

Shake first four ingredients and strain into a Collins glass over ice. Garnish with an orange slice.

Electric Screwdriver

2 oz. orange juice
1 oz. energy drink
¾ oz. Jose Cuervo Especial Gold tequila
¾ oz. Smirnoff Red Label vodka
Ice cubes
Orange slice for garnish

Build in a glass half-filled with ice. Garnish with
an orange slice.

Eliminator

6 oz. orange soda
1 ½ oz. Wild Turkey 101 bourbon
1 ½ oz. Jose Cuervo tequila

Mix all ingredients in a tall glass.

Exorcist

2 ½ oz. tequila
¾ oz. blue curaçao
¾ oz. lime juice
Dash Tabasco sauce
Ice cubes

Shake and strain into a cocktail glass.

Freddy Fudpucker

4 oz. orange juice
2 oz. tequila
Ice cubes
½ oz. Galliano for float

Pour first two ingredients into a highball glass almost filled with ice cubes. Pour slowly and carefully over the back of a teaspoon. Float the Galliano on top of the drink.

Froggy Potion

1 oz. gin
1 oz. Jose Cuervo tequila
1 oz. rum
1 oz. vodka
Dash cola
Ice cubes
Orange juice to fill

Pour first five ingredients into a glass with ice and fill with orange juice.

Frostbite

2 oz. Jose Cuervo tequila
1 oz. lemon-lime soda
¼ cup lime sherbert

Blend. Remove carefully.

Garter Belt

1 oz. heavy cream
1 oz. Patrón XO Café tequila
1 oz. white crème de cacao
Ice cubes
Ground espresso for garnish
Shaved chocolate for garnish

Shake first three ingredients with ice until well blended. Strain into a chilled cocktail glass. Garnish with a sprinkle of ground espresso and chocolate.

The Giraffe

2 oz. tequila
½ oz. St. Germain Elderflower liqueur
2 ice cubes
3 oz. grapefruit juice

Pour the first two ingredients into a tall glass, followed by the two ice cubes. Swirl the two around in the glass for a time (note: do not stir), and then add grapefruit juice.

Golddigger

1 ½ oz. Jose Cuervo Especial Gold tequila
½ oz. lime juice
½ oz. triple sec
Dash grenadine
Ice cubes

Shake first four ingredients with ice and serve on the rocks or as a shot.

Golden Eye

1 ½ oz. Jose Cuervo Especial Gold tequila
½ oz. peppermint schnapps

Serve on the rocks or straight up.

Golden Iguana

1 ½ oz. Jose Cuervo Especial Gold tequila
1 ½ oz. orange juice
1 ½ oz. pineapple juice
Ice cubes

Pour first three ingredients over ice and stir.

Grape Ape

4 oz. white grape juice
2 oz. tequila
White grape for garnish

Shake with ice and pour into a highball glass over ice. Garnish with a white grape.

Green Lizard

1 oz. tequila
½ oz. green crème de menthe
½ oz. St. Germain Elderflower liqueur

A weaker tequila drink for the beginner tequila drinkers.

Headcrush

2 oz. Jose Cuervo tequila
½ oz. Tabasco green pepper sauce
Whipped cream to top
Salt to taste

Pour tequila into a glass, and then add Tabasco sauce carefully. Top with whipped cream and add some salt.

Heavenly Billionaire's Margarita

2 oz. Gran Centenario Añejo tequila
1 ½ oz. fresh-squeezed lime juice
1 oz. Gran Marnier Cuvée du Cent
    Cinquantenaire liqueur
½ orange wheel for garnish

Shake vigorously with ice and strain into a pre-chilled martini glass. Garnish with half an orange wheel.

Hoo Hoo

1 ½ oz. Midori Melon liqueur
1 ½ oz. tequila
½ oz. grenadine
Ice cubes
Melon ball for garnish (optional)

Shake first three ingredients with ice and strain into a martini glass. Garnish with a small melon ball, if desired.

Hot Apple Rose

2 oz. Tequila Rose
Hot apple cider to fill
Whipped cream

Pour tequila into a mug and fill with hot apple cider. Garnish with whipped cream.

Hot Chocolate Rose

1 ½ oz. Tequila Rose
Hot chocolate to fill

Pour Tequila Rose into a mug and fill with hot chocolate.

Hot Shot

1 beef bouillon cube
Boiling water
1 ½ oz. Jose Cuervo Tequila
Salt and pepper to taste

Dissolve the cube of beef bouillon in a mug of boiling water. Add the tequila and season to taste.

Hot 'T'

2 oz. Tarantula Reposado tequila
3 dashes Tabasco sauce

Serve as a shot.

Hottie

2 oz. milk
2 oz. Patrón tequila
1 tbsp. dark chocolate, melted
4 dashes Tabasco Habanero Pepper sauce
½ oz. Grand Marnier
Maraschino cherry for garnish

Shake the first four ingredients with ice and pour in a cognac glass. Or, heat the first four ingredients in the microwave and pour into a cognac glass for a warm drink. Float the Grand Marnier and garnish with a cherry.

Hot to Trot

½ oz. DeKuyper Hot Damn Cinnamon schnapps
½ oz. Jose Cuervo tequila
Dash lime juice

Rim a shooter glass with lime and salt and pour the first two ingredients in. Add a dash of lime juice and SLAM!

In Cuervogue

2 oz. Jose Cuervo Especial Gold tequila
1 maraschino cherry for garnish

Serve in a brandy snifter.

Inoculation Shot

1 oz. blue curaçao
1 oz. Jose Cuervo Especial Gold tequila

Serve in a shot glass.

Jellybean

Splash grenadine
½ oz. sambuca
½ oz. Jose Cuervo tequila

Layer.

Jellyfish

½ oz. white sambuca
½ oz. white tequila
Drop Tabasco sauce

Pour first two ingredients into a shot glass and top with 1 drop of Tabasco.

José and Pepe

½ part Chambord
½ part Jose Cuervo Especial Gold tequila

Serve in a shot glass.

Jumping Bean

1 ½ oz. Jose Cuervo tequila
½ oz. sambuca
3 coffee beans

Shake first two ingredients with ice and strain drink into a cocktail glass. Drop coffee beans into middle of drink, and serve.

Key Lime Tini

1 oz. El Mayor Reposado tequila
½ oz. heavy cream
½ oz. KeKe Beach Key Lime liqueur
½ oz. Rose's Lime Juice
½ oz. TUACA Vanilla Cream liqueur

Shake well with ice and strain into chilled martini glass.

La Bomba

1 ½ oz. orange juice
1 ½ oz. pineapple juice
1 ¼ oz. 1800 tequila
¾ oz. Cointreau
2 dashes grenadine
Lime wheel for garnish

Coat glass rim with sugar. Shake all ingredients
with ice until slushy and frothy. Serve in a salt-
rimmed glass. Garnish with a lime wheel.

Ladies Night

1 oz. amaretto or Frangelico liqueur
1 oz. Patrón XO Café tequila
1 oz. Stolichnaya Vanilla vodka
Ice cubes
Coffee beans for garnish

Shake first three ingredients well with ice and
strain into a chilled martini glass. Garnish with
coffee beans.

Latin Lover

1 ½ oz. tequila
¾ oz. amaretto
Ice cubes

Pour first two ingredients into an old-fashioned glass and fill with ice.

Lizard Juice

½ oz. freshly squeezed orange juice
½ oz. pineapple juice
½ oz. Jose Cuervo Especial Gold tequila
Ice cubes
Blue curaçao for float
Orange slice for garnish

Combine first three ingredients in a rocks glass with ice. Float blue curaçao. Garnish with the orange slice.

Lolita

2 oz. tequila
⅓ oz. lime juice
1 tsp. honey
2 dashes Angostura bitters
Ice cubes

Shake and strain over one or two ice cubes in a cocktail glass.

Long Island Iced Tea

¼ oz. gin
¼ oz. tequila
¼ oz. vodka
¼ oz. whiskey
¼ oz. white rum
1 oz. simple syrup
Orange juice to fill
Splash cola

Mix alcohol in large glass, add syrup, and fill with orange juice. Add a splash of cola for color.

Low Rider

1 ½ oz. Jose Cuervo Especial Gold tequila
½ oz. triple sec
Splash cranberry juice

Shake with ice and serve in a shot glass.

Massacre

2 oz. tequila
1 tsp. Campari
Ice cubes
4 oz. ginger ale

Pour the first two ingredients into a highball glass over ice and top with ginger ale. Stir well.

Merry Widow

3 oz. champagne
1 oz. Jose Cuervo Especial Gold tequila
Splash orange juice
Orange wheel for garnish

Serve in a champagne glass. Garnish with the orange wheel.

Mexican Flag

1 shot crème de menthe
1 shot white tequila
1 shot grenadine

Layer the shots in order of the colors of the Mexican flag.

Mexican High Dive

2 oz. tequila
1 raw oyster
Drop Tabasco Chipotle Pepper sauce
Ice cubes

Pour first three ingredients into a glass with ice.

Mexican Witch

1 ½ oz. tequila
¾ oz. Strega liqueur
Ice cubes

Pour first two ingredients into an old-fashioned glass over ice.

Mexicola

2 oz. tequila
Juice ½ lime
Cola to fill

Pour tequila and lime juice over ice cubes in a Collins glass. Fill with cola and stir.

Mockingbird

1 ¼ oz. Pepe Lopez Gold Tequila
1 oz. fresh lime juice
2 tsp. white crème de menthe

Shake vigorously and strain into a chilled martini glass.

Moonraker

4 oz. pineapple juice
1 ½ oz. tequila
½ oz. blue curaçao

Serve in a tall glass.

Need for Speed

3 oz. lemon-lime soda
2 oz. tequila
Ice cubes

Pour first two ingredients into a tall glass over ice.

Old-Fashioned

1 tsp. sugar
5 dashes Angostura bitters
¼ oz. sparkling water
Ice cubes
2 oz. tequila
Maraschino cherries for garnish

Combine sugar, bitters, and water in the bottom of a chilled old-fashioned glass. Fill with ice and add tequila. Stir well. Drop in a cherry or two.

Paloma

Lime wedge for rim
Course salt for rim
3 oz. grapefruit juice
2 oz. Jose Cuervo Tradicional tequila
Ice cubes

Rub rim of a tall glass with lime and dip into salt. Mix remaining ingredients and pour into the garnished glass.

Patron Perfect Cosmo

2 oz. Patrón Silver tequila
¾ oz. Patrón Citronge Orange liqueur
Splash cranberry juice
Lime squeeze
Lime wheel for garnish

Shake well with ice and strain into a martini glass. Garnish with a lime wheel.

Pepperita

Course salt for rim
Lime wedge for rim
Ice cubes
1 ¼ oz. Jose Cuervo Especial Gold tequila
⅔ oz. Grand Marnier
Juice ½ lime
1 tsp. Tabasco green pepper sauce
Lime slice for garnish

Rub the rim of a goblet with the cut side of a lime.
Dip rim into a saucer of salt. Fill glass with ice.
Pour tequila, Grand Marnier, and lime juice into
an ice-filled cocktail shaker or pitcher, and shake
or stir vigorously. Strain into ice-filled glasses.
Shake in pepper sauce and stir. Garnish with a
slice of lime.

Pick Me Up Jose

1 oz. Jose Cuervo Especial Gold tequila
½ oz. Captain Morgan rum

Serve in a shot glass.

Pink Cad

1 ½ oz. 1800 tequila
Ice cubes
½ oz. triple sec
4 oz. Jose Cuervo Margarita Mix
½ oz. Grand Marnier
1 oz. fresh lime juice

Pour tequila over ice. Add triple sec, margarita mix, Grand Marnier, and fresh juice. Stir gently and serve.

Pink Panther

2 oz. cream or half-and-half
1 ½ oz. Buen Amigo tequila
½ oz. grenadine
Ice cubes

Blend and strain. Pour into chilled cocktail glass.

Pink Spider

1 ¼ oz. Tarantula Azul Tequila liqueur
1 oz. pineapple juice
1 oz. pink grapefruit juice
½ oz. grenadine
1 squeeze of ¼ lime
Ice cubes
Lime slice for garnish

Shake first five ingredients vigorously with ice and strain into glass with ice. Garnish with a lime slice.

Praying Mantis

4 oz. cola
1 ½ oz. Jose Cuervo Especial Gold tequila
2 tsp. lime juice
1 tsp. lemon juice
Ice cubes

Serve in a tall glass with ice.

Prickly Agave

1 ½ oz. fresh sweet-and-sour
1 ½ oz. Patrón Silver tequila
1 oz. prickly pear puree
½ oz. Patron Citronge Orange liqueur
Malibu Caribbean Mango rum to float
Lemon wheel for garnish

Shake with ice and serve straight up or on the rocks. Garnish with a lemon wheel.

Pulco

2 oz. Jose Cuervo 1800 tequila
1 ½ oz. lime juice
½ oz. Cointreau
Splash orange juice
Ice cubes

Serve on the rocks. Do not shake.

Quick Silver

1 oz. anisette
1 oz. Jose Cuervo tequila
1 oz. triple sec

Serve in a lowball glass.

Red Beard

2 oz. cranberry juice
2 oz. tequila
½ oz. sloe gin

Stir in a highball glass.

Rose Bud

1 ½ oz. Tequila Rose
½ oz. coconut rum

Serve in a shot glass.

Rosita

1 ½ oz. tequila
1 oz. Campari
½ oz. dry vermouth
½ oz. sweet vermouth
Crushed ice

Pour over crushed ice and stir well.

Scorpion's Sting

½ oz. rum
½ oz. tequila
Splash Tabasco Chipotle pepper sauce

Serve in a shot glass.

Sexy Lemonade

1 oz. triple sec
½ oz. 1800 tequila
½ oz. lemon-lime soda
Sweet-and-sour mix to fill
Sugar to taste
Lemon slice for garnish

Pour first three ingredients into an ice-filled highball glass. Fill with sweet-and-sour and add sugar. Drop in a slice of lemon and stir well.

Shark Attack

1 ½ oz. tequila
½ oz. Cointreau
½ oz. sloe gin
Coarse sugar for rim

Shake and strain. Serve as a shot with sugared rim.

Silk Panty Raid

1 oz. cranberry juice
1 oz. peach schnapps
1 oz. tequila

Stir with ice and serve in a chilled cocktail glass.

Silver Devil

1 oz. peppermint schnapps
1 oz. tequila

Layer in a shot glass.

Sloe Tequila

1 oz. tequila
½ oz. sloe gin
1 tbsp. lime juice
½ cup ice
Cucumber peel twist for garnish

Blend with ice at low speed and pour into an old-fashioned glass. Garnish with a twist of cucumber peel.

Snake Bite

1 oz. Jack Daniel's Tennessee Whisky
1 oz. tequila

An excellent drink, but like the name, it has a bite!

Southern Tradition Margarita

5 oz. sweet-and-sour mix
1 ½ oz. Jose Cuervo Tradicional tequila
½ oz. fresh orange juice
½ oz. Southern Comfort bourbon
Ice cubes

Shake with ice and serve.

Spider Bite

8.5 oz. can Red Bull
1 ½ oz. Tarantula Azul tequila
Ice cubes

Serve in a 14-oz. glass over ice.

Stinger Tequila

2 parts tequila
2 parts white crème de menthe
Ice cubes

Shake well and strain into a chilled martini glass.

Sunburn

1 oz. Cointreau
1 oz. tequila
Cranberry juice to fill
Ice cubes

Pour into a Collins glass with ice and enjoy.

Sunstroke

2 oz. pineapple juice
1 ¾ oz. Jose Cuervo Tradicional tequila
½ oz. lime juice
¼ oz. Cointreau
Ice cubes

Serve on the rocks.

Tarantula Bite

3 oz. sweet-and-sour mix
1 ½ oz. Tarantula Azul tequila
½ oz. fresh lime juice
½ oz. triple sec
Ice cubes
Splash grenadine
Lime wedge for garnish

Shake first four ingredients vigorously with ice and pour into a 14-oz. Collins glass. Top with about ⅛ oz. grenadine and garnish with a lime wedge.

Tarantula Crandaddy

5 oz. cranberry juice
1 oz. McCormick triple sec
1 oz. Tarantula Plata tequila
Ice cubes

Pour first three ingredients in a large glass over ice. Stir.

Tarantula Slammer

1 oz. lemon-lime soda
½ oz. Tarantula Reposado tequila

Serve as a shot.

Teq and Tea

6 oz. sweetened iced tea
1 ½ oz. tequila
Ice cubes

Mix first two ingredients over ice.

Tequil O'Neil

1 ¼ oz. Jose Cuervo Especial Gold tequila
¼ oz. orange juice
⅛ oz. club soda

Serve in shot glass covered with a basketball-type coaster and slam.

Tequila Amigo

1 oz. Jose Cuervo Especial Gold tequila
½ oz. Godiva Cappucino liqueur
1 oz. heavy cream

Layer in a shot glass.

Tequila Fire "33"

3 oz. tequila
3 drops Tabasco sauce
Club soda to fill

Stir first two ingredients in a highball glass and add club soda to put out the fire.

Tequila Fizz

2 oz. tequila
1 tbsp. lemon juice
¾ oz. grenadine
½ oz. lime juice
Ice cubes
Ginger ale to fill

Shake first four ingredients with ice and strain into a Collins glass over ice cubes. Fill with ginger ale and stir.

Tequila Manhattan

2 oz. tequila
1 oz. sweet vermouth
Splash lime juice
Ice cubes
Maraschino cherry for garnish
Orange slice for garnish

Shake first three ingredients with ice and strain into an old-fashioned glass over ice cubes. Garnish with the cherry and orange slice.

Tequila Matador

3 oz. pineapple juice
1 ½ oz. Oro Azul Blanco tequila
Juice ½ lime

Shake all ingredients in a cocktail shaker with ice. Strain into a champagne flute and serve.

Tequila Mockingbird

1 ½ oz. tequila
1 oz. lime juice or juice ½ lime
1 oz. white crème de menthe

Shake well with ice and strain into a cocktail glass.

Tequila Mojito

2 sugar cubes
1-2 fresh basil leaves
1 ½ oz. Oro Azul Blanco tequila
3 oz. fresh lime juice
Ice cubes

Grind the sugar cubes and basil leaves in a cocktail shaker. Add tequila and lime juice. Shake until blended, and pour into a Collins glass with ice.

Tequila Paralyzer

1 oz. Kahlúa
1 oz. tequila
Splash milk
Cola to fill
Heavy cream to taste

Build first three ingredients in a highball glass. Fill with cola and top with heavy cream.

Tequila Sour

2 oz. lemon juice
1 ½ oz. tequila
1 tsp. sugar
Crushed ice
Maraschino cherry for garnish

Blend first three ingredients with crushed ice and strain into a sour glass. Garnish with a red cherry. Use añejo for a better taste.

Tequila Sunrise

4 oz. orange juice
2 oz. ice-cold tequila
¼ oz. grenadine

Pour orange juice into a highball glass and then pour in the ice-cold tequila slowly, tilting the glass to get a layered effect. Trickle grenadine on top. This should result in a perfect sunrise. Garnish with a stirrer and straw.

Tequila Sunset

2 parts grapefruit juice
1 part ice-cold tequila
1 part grenadine

Pour grapefruit juice into a highball glass and then pour in tequila slowly, tilting the glass for a layered effect. Trickle grenadine on top. This should result in a perfect sunset. Garnish with a stirrer, straw, and grapefruit slice or cherry. Instead of ice-cold tequila you can use ice cubes.

Tequini

1 ½ oz. premium silver tequila
½ oz. dry vermouth
Ice cubes
Lime twist or jalapeño-stuffed olive for garnish

A premium tequila will give any vodka or gin competition in this upscale Mexican martini. Briefly stir tequila and vermouth over cracked ice in a mixing glass until chilled. Strain ice and pour immediately into a chilled 3-oz. martini glass. Garnish with a twist of lime peel or a jalapeno-stuffed olive.

Tijuana Taxi

2 oz. gold tequila
1 oz. blue curaçao
1 oz. tropical fruit schnapps
Lemon-lime soda to fill
Orange slice for garnish
Maraschino cherry for garnish

Build first three ingredients in a highball glass and fill with lemon-lime soda. Garnish with an orange slice and a cherry.

Tijuana Tea

3 oz. cola
1 oz. sweet-and-sour mix
¾ oz. 1800 tequila
¾ oz. Jose Cuervo Especial Gold tequila
½ oz. triple sec
Ice cubes
Lime slice for garnish
Maraschino cherry for garnish

Combine first five ingredients in a tall glass with ice. Garnish with lime slice and a cherry.

TNT (Cuervo Gold Tequila 'N' Tonic)

4 oz. tonic
1 ½ oz. Jose Cuervo Especial Gold tequila
½ cup ice
Splash lime juice
Lime for garnish

Pour the tonic and tequila into a 10-oz. footed highball glass, and add the ice. Mix in lime juice. Garnish with a lime.

Toreador

1 ½ oz. light cream
1 ½ oz. tequila
½ oz. crème de cacao
Whipped cream for garnish
Sprinkle of cocoa for garnish

Shake with ice and strain into a cocktail glass. Garnish with whipped cream and a sprinkle of cocoa.

The Ultimate Shot

½ oz. 1800 tequila
½ oz. Grand Marnier

Serve in a shot glass.

Untamed Margarita

2 ½ oz. sweet-and-sour mix
1 oz. Jose Cuervo Especial Gold tequila
½ oz. fresh lime juice
½ oz. triple sec
Ice cubes
Blue curaçao for float
Lime slice for garnish
Maraschino cherry for garnish

Combine first four ingredients in shaker with ice
and strain into cocktail glass. Float blue curaçao
and garnish with lime and a cherry.

White Cactus

1 oz. tequila
Ginger ale to taste
Splash lime juice
Ice cubes
Lime slice for garnish

Pour first three ingredients into a highball glass
over ice and garnish with a slice of lime.

Wild Rose

2 parts McCormick's Irish Cream liqueur
2 parts Tequila Rose
1 part Polar Ice vodka
Ice cubes

Shake well and serve on the rocks.

Wild Thing

1 ½ oz. tequila
1 oz. club soda
1 oz. cranberry juice
Ice cubes
½ oz. lime juice
Lime wedge for garnish

Pour first three ingredients over ice into an old-fashioned glass. Garnish with a lime wedge.

Yellow Devil Margarita

3 oz. sweet-and-sour mix
1 ½ oz. Jose Cuervo Tradicional tequila
¾ oz. Cointreau
¼ oz. Galliano
Ice cubes

Serve on the rocks.

Yvette

2 oz. heavy cream
2 oz. tequila
1 oz. apricot brandy
Sprite to fill

Mix first three ingredients in a highball glass and fill with Sprite.

Zipper

1 ½ oz. Cointreau
1 ½ oz. tequila
½ oz. cream

Layer in a lowball glass.

VODKA

The Vodka Martini

1 ½ oz. Absolut vodka
Dash extra dry vermouth
Lemon twist or olives for garnish

Stir (or shake, if you wish) in a cocktail shaker with ice. Strain and serve straight up in a cocktail glass or on the rocks. Garnish with the lemon twist or olives.

. . .

Cornet
Replace the extra dry vermouth with your favorite port wine, be it ruby, tawny, etc.

Dillatini
Garnish with a dilly bean (try to find one).

Fascinator
Add a dash of Pernod and a sprig of mint.

Gibson
Add a pickled cocktail onion.

Gimlet
Replace the extra dry vermouth with Rose's lime juice and garnish with a slice of lime.

Gypsy
Add a maraschino cherry.

Homestead

Add an orange slice.

Italian

Replace the extra dry vermouth with amaretto.

Jackson

Replace the extra dry vermouth with Dubonnet and a dash of bitters.

Lone Tree

Add a dash of lemon juice.

Mickey Finn

Add a splash of white crème de menthe and garnish with a sprig of mint.

Naked Martini

Just Absolut Vodka.

Nave Cocktail

Replace the extra dry vermouth with Rosso sweet vermouth. Add a cocktail onion and a twist of lemon peel.

Orangetini

Add a splash of triple sec and a twist of orange peel.

Perfection

Replace the extra dry vermouth with Rosso sweet vermouth.

Plaza

Replace half of the extra dry vermouth with Rosso sweet vermouth.

Queen Elizabeth

Add a splash of Benedictine.

Richmond

Replace the extra dry vermouth with Lillet and add a twist of lemon peel.

Rosa

Add ⅛ oz. cherry brandy.

Rosalind Russell

Replace the extra dry vermouth with aquavit.

Roselyn

Add ⅛ oz. grenadine and a lemon twist.

Saketini

Replace the extra dry vermouth with sake.

Smoky Martini

Replace the vermouth with The Glenlivet.

Sour Kisses

Add an egg white and shake (do not stir) vigorously. (Egg whites and raw eggs are forbidden in some states and towns. Check your local board of health. They can be replaced with the Original Frothee where available.)

Trinity (aka Trio)

Replace the extra dry vermouth with a small dash of Rosso sweet vermouth.

Velocity

Add an orange slice and shake. Remove orange and garnish with a fresh orange slice.

Wallick

Add a dash of curaçao.

Warden

Add a dash of Pernod.

Absolut and Tonic

1 ¼ oz. Absolut vodka
Ice cubes
Tonic to fill
Lime wedge for garnish

Pour the vodka over ice in a tall glass. Fill with tonic and garnish with lime wedge.

Absolut Collins

1 ¼ oz. Absolut vodka
¾ oz. sweetened lemon mix
Ice cubes
Club soda to fill

Shake the vodka and lemon mix with ice and pour into a tall glass with ice. Top with club soda.

Absolut Cooler

½ tsp. superfine sugar
2 oz. club soda
Ice cubes
1 ¼ oz. Absolut vodka
Ginger ale or carbonated water
Spiral of orange or lemon peel (or both) for
    garnish

Stir the superfine sugar with club soda. Fill a
glass with ice and add vodka. Top with ginger
ale or carbonated water and stir again. Dangle
garnish over rim of glass.

Absolut Gimlet

1 ¼ oz. Absolut vodka
½ oz. fresh lime juice
Ice cubes
Lime twist for garnish

Stir the vodka and lime juice in a shaker glass
with ice. Strain into a cocktail glass.

Absolution

2 oz. chilled Absolut vodka
Chilled Mumm champagne to fill
Lemon slice for halo garnish

Pour the chilled vodka and champagne into a champagne flute. Cut a lemon peel in the form of a ring to represent a halo. The lemon peel can be either wrapped around the top of the glass or floated on top of the cocktail.

Absolut Seabreeze

1 ¼ oz. Absolut vodka
Ice cubes
Grapefruit juice
Cranberry juice to fill

Pour the vodka over ice in a tall glass. Fill halfway with grapefruit juice and top it off with cranberry juice.

Absolut Transfusion

1 ¼ oz. Absolut vodka
Ice cubes
½ oz. grape juice
Club soda to fill

Pour the vodka over ice in a tall glass and add grape juice. Top with club soda.

Absolut White Russian

1 oz. Absolut vodka
½ oz. Godiva Chocolate liqueur
½ oz. heavy cream
Ice cubes

Pour the vodka, Godiva liqueur, and cream over ice in a rocks glass. Shake and serve.

Alabama Slammer

¾ oz. amaretto
¾ oz. Southern Comfort bourbon
¾ oz. vodka
Dash sloe gin or grenadine
Orange juice to fill
Orange slice for garnish

Pour first four ingredients into a glass filled with ice. Fill with orange juice. Shake. Garnish with an orange slice.

Almond Lemonade

1 ¼ oz. vodka
¼ oz. crème de noyaux
½ oz. lemonade
Lemon slice for garnish

Pour the vodka and crème de noyaux over ice in a tall glass. Add the lemonade and garnish with the lemon slice.

Anti-Freeze

2 oz. vodka
½ oz. Midori Melon liqueur

Shake with ice and strain into a glass.

Apple Joll-E Rancher

2 oz. sour mix
1 ½ oz. vodka
½ oz. sour apple schnapps
Ice cubes
Lemon-lime soda to fill

Shake first three ingredients with ice and fill with lemon-lime soda.

Appletini

2 oz. SKYY vodka
1 oz. sour apple liqueur
Splash lemon-lime soda

Apryski

1 ½ oz. Sobieski vodka
½ oz. Marie Brizard Apry liqueur
Ice cubes

Shake and serve over ice or as a shot.

Aqueduct

¾ oz. Ultimat vodka
¼ oz. brandy
¼ oz. triple sec
½ tbsp. lime juice

Shake all ingredients with ice in a shaker glass.
Strain into chilled cocktail glass.

Banana Boomer

1 ½ oz. Smirnoff vodka
½ oz. crème de banana

Shake both ingredients with ice. Serve straight up or on the rocks.

Banana Cream Pie Martini

2 ½ oz. vodka
Dash banana liqueur
Dash Irish cream

Shake with ice and strain into chilled glass.

Banana Split

2 oz. Sobieski vodka
½ oz. crème de banana
½ oz. white crème de cacao
½ oz. Baileys Crème Caramel

Shake.

 JOSEPH GERMANO

Bay Breeze

2 oz. SKYY vodka
1 oz. cranberry juice
1 oz. pineapple juice

Beach Bum

1 ½ oz. Midori Melon liqueur
1 oz. cranberry juice
1 oz. Sobieski vodka

Shake with ice and strain into a cocktail glass.

Berry Lemonade

1 oz. Sobieski vodka
½ oz. lemonade
¼ oz. strawberry liqueur
Ice cubes
Fresh strawberry for garnish

Pour first three ingredients over ice in a tall glass
and garnish with a strawberry.

Bert Simpsin

½ oz. coconut rum
½ oz. melon liqueur
½ oz. vodka

Shake with ice. Strain into a chilled glass.

Bikini Line

¾ oz. coffee liqueur
¾ oz. raspberry liqueur
¾ oz. vodka
Ice cubes

Pour first three ingredients into a glass over ice.

Black Eye

1 ½ oz. Ketel One vodka
½ oz. blackberry brandy
Ice cubes

Stir. Serve straight up or on the rocks.

Black Orchid

1 ½ oz. cranberry juice
1 oz. Sobieski vodka
½ oz. blue curaçao
Ice cubes

Build over ice in a 7-oz. rocks glass.

Black Russian

1 oz. Smirnoff vodka
¼ oz. Kahlúa
Ice cubes
Lemon twist for garnish

Shake first two ingredients with ice and strain into a cocktail glass. Garnish with the lemon twist.

Blood Orange

2 oz. SKYY vodka
1 oz. Campari
Orange juice
Orange slice for garnish

Build in a glass and fill with orange juice. Garnish with a slice of orange.

Bloody Bull

1 ½ oz. beef bouillon
1 ½ oz. tomato juice
1 ¼ oz. Sobieski vodka
1–2 tsp. lemon juice
Dash Tabasco sauce
Dash Worcestershire sauce
Ice cubes
Freshly ground black pepper to taste

Shake the first six ingredients with ice in a shaker. Strain into an old-fashioned glass and add pepper.

Bloody Caesar

3 oz. Clamato juice
1 ¼ oz. Sobieski vodka
Ice cubes
Dash Tabasco sauce
Dash Worcestershire sauce
Dash pepper
Dash salt
Celery stalk or lime wheel for garnish

Build over ice. Add dash of Tabasco, Worcestershire, pepper, and salt. Garnish with celery stalk or lime wheel.

Bloody Delicious

2 parts tomato juice
2 parts UV vodka
1 part celery salt
1 part Tabasco sauce
1 part Worcestershire sauce
Ice cubes

Serve over ice in a highball glass.

Bloody Maria

4 oz. tomato juice
2 oz. SKYY vodka
1 ½ tsp. fresh lime juice
1 tsp. dry sherry
¼ tsp. celery salt or seeds
¼ tsp. Frank's Redhot Original Cayenne
    Pepper sauce
¼ tsp. Worcestershire Sauce
Coarsely ground black pepper and salt to
    taste

Bloody Mary

3 oz. tomato juice
1 ½ oz. vodka
1-2 tsp. lemon juice
Dash Tabasco sauce
Dash Worcestershire sauce
Freshly ground black pepper

Combine in a shaker. Strain into a chilled old-fashioned glass and add pepper to taste.

Blue Hawaiian

1 ½ oz. vodka
½ oz. blue curaçao
Ice cubes
Orange juice
Pineapple juice
Pineapple spear for garnish

Pour first two ingredients into a glass over ice and fill with equal parts orange and pineapple juice. Shake. Garnish with pineapple spear.

Blue Lagoon

1 oz. vodka
½ oz. pineapple juice
¼ oz. blue curaçao
Dash bitters
Ice cubes
Lemon peel for garnish

Combine first four ingredients in shaker with ice. Strain into a chilled cocktail glass. Twist lemon peel over drink and add.

Blue Monday

1 oz. Ketel One vodka
¼ oz. triple sec
Dash blue curaçao
Ice cubes

Combine first three ingredients with ice in a shaker. Strain into a chilled cocktail glass.

Bocce Ball

1 ¼ oz. Grey Goose vodka
1 oz. orange juice
¾ oz. Amaretto di Saronno
Ice cubes

Shake all ingredients. Serve straight up or on the rocks.

Brass Monkey

2 oz. light rum
2 oz. SKYY vodka
Orange juice

Pour first two ingredients into a glass and fill with orange juice.

Brown Derby

1 ¼ oz. Ultimat vodka
Ice cubes
Cola to fill

Pour the vodka in a tall glass with ice and top with cola.

Cape Codder

3 oz. cranberry juice
1 ¼ oz. Ultimat vodka
Dash lime juice
Ice cubes

Shake and strain into a chilled cocktail glass.

Cheap Sunglasses

2 oz. vodka
Ice cubes
Cranberry juice
Lemon-lime soda
Pineapple spear for garnish

Pour vodka into a glass over ice and fill with equal parts cranberry juice and lemon-lime soda. Garnish with the pineapple.

Cheesecake Martini

¾ oz. Smirnoff strawberry vodka
¾ oz. Smirnoff vanilla vodka
Splash cranberry juice
Ice cubes

Shake and strain into a martini glass.

Chi Chi

1 ½ oz. cream of coconut
1 ½ oz. Sobieski vodka
¾ oz. pineapple juice
Ice cubes
Maraschino cherry for garnish

Combine first three ingredients with ice in a blender and serve in a rocks glass. Garnish with the cherry.

Chocolate Chip

2 oz. SKYY vodka, chilled
½ oz. Frangelico liqueur

Chocolate Thunder

2 oz. Sobieski vodka
Chocolate milk

Pour vodka into a glass and fill with chocolate milk.

Cloudy Night

1 part Grey Goose vodka
1 part Tia Maria
Ice cubes

Stir on the rocks.

Colorado Mother

2 oz. vodka
¾ oz. coffee liqueur
¾ oz. tequila
Milk or cream
Galliano

Pour first three ingredients into a glass over ice and
fill with milk or cream. Shake. Top with Galliano.

Comfortable Screw

1 oz. Southern Comfort bourbon
1 oz. vodka
Ice cubes
Orange juice

Pour first two ingredients into a glass with ice and fill with orange juice.

Copperhead

2 oz. Smirnoff vodka
Ice cubes
1 lime wedge, plus one for garnish
3 oz. ginger ale to fill

Pour the vodka into a tall glass filled with ice and squeeze in the juice of one lime wedge. Fill with ginger ale. Garnish with the remaining lime wedge.

Dirty Martini

2 oz. SKYY vodka
¼ oz. olive juice

Stir. Serve in a chilled martini glass.

Dirty Monkey

¾ oz. banana liqueur
¾ oz. coffee liqueur
¾ oz. vodka
½ scoop vanilla ice cream

Blend until smooth.

Fuzzy Martini

2 oz. SKYY vodka
1 oz. peach schnapps
Splash orange juice

Fuzzy Navel

4 oz. Tropicana orange juice
2 oz. DeKuyper peach schnapps
Ice cubes

Pour first two ingredients into a highball glass
filled with ice. Stir.

Fuzzy Navel with Vodka

2 oz. SKYY vodka
1 oz. peach schnapps
Orange juice to fill

Pour first two ingredients into a glass and fill with orange juice.

Godchild

2 oz. Sobieski vodka
1 oz. amaretto
1 oz. heavy cream

Godmother

1 oz. Grey Goose vodka
¼ oz. Amaretto di Saronno

Serve in a rocks glass over ice.

Greyhound

1 ¼ oz. vodka
Ice cubes
Grapefruit juice to fill

Pour the vodka in a tall glass with ice and add grapefruit juice.

Harvey Wallbanger

4 oz. orange juice
1 ½ oz. vodka
Ice cubes
½ oz. Galliano

Combine the orange juice and vodka in a high-ball glass filled with ice. Stir. Float the Galliano on top.

Hop-Skip-and-Go-Naked

1 oz. Bombay gin
1 oz. SKYY vodka
Juice ½ lime
Ice cubes
Budweiser beer to fill

Combine gin, vodka, and lime juice in a mug over ice. Top with Budweiser.

Horseshot

4 oz. tomato juice
1 ¼ oz. horseradish
1 ¼ oz. Sobieski vodka
Celery stalk for garnish

Serve over ice in a cocktail glass. Garnish with a celery stalk.

Ice Pick

1 ¼ oz. SKYY vodka
Lemon iced tea
Ice cubes
Lemon slice for garnish

Pour vodka and iced tea over ice in a tall glass.
Garnish with the lemon.

Imperial Czar

¼ oz. triple sec
¼ oz. Stolichnaya vodka
Dash lime juice
Dash orange bitters
¾ oz. dry sparkling wine

Combine all ingredients except wine in a shaker
with ice. Strain into a chilled wine glass. Top with
the wine and stir.

Kamikaze

1 ½ oz. Stolichnaya vodka
Splash Cointreau
Splash lime juice

Combine all ingredients and shake well with ice.
Strain into a shot glass or on the rocks.

Kremlin Colonel

1 ¼ oz. Stolichnaya vodka
2 tbsp. sugar syrup
3-4 mint leaves torn in half for garnish

Combine in a shaker with ice. Strain into a cock-tail glass.

Madras

1 ¼ oz. vodka
Ice cubes
Cranberry juice
Orange juice

Pour vodka into a tall glass over ice and fill with equal parts cranberry juice and orange juice.

Martini (Vodka)

2 ¼ oz. vodka
Dash of extra dry vermouth
Lemon twist or olive for garnish

Shake or stir well over ice and strain into a cocktail glass straight up or over ice. Garnish with a lemon twist or an olive.

Meat and Potato Martini

2 ½ oz. Teton Glacier potato vodka
Splash dry vermouth
Sausage or pepperoni slice for garnish

Shake with ice and strain into a martini glass.
Garnish with a slice of sausage or pepperoni.

Melon Ball

1 oz. melon liqueur
½ oz. vodka
Ice cubes
Orange juice
Pineapple juice

Pour first two ingredients into a glass over ice
and fill with equal parts orange juice and pineapple juice.

Midnight Martini

1 oz. 360 vodka
¼ oz. Kahlúa
Ice cubes
Lemon twist for garnish

Combine the 360 vodka and Kahlúa in a shaker
with ice. Strain into a cocktail glass and garnish
with lemon twist.

Mudslide

1 oz. Carolans Irish cream liqueur
1 oz. coffee liqueur
1 oz. SKYY vodka
Ice cubes

Shake. Serve over rocks.

Negroni (Vodka)

½ oz. Campari
½ oz. SKYY Vodka
½ oz. sweet vermouth
Ice cubes
Orange slice for garnish

Stir together on the rocks.

Panzer

1 oz. Bombay gin
1 oz. triple sec
1 oz. Ultimat vodka

Combine in a shaker with ice. Strain into a chilled cocktail glass.

Pink Baby

2 oz. SKYY vodka
1 oz. cherry liqueur
1 oz. sweet-and-sour mix

Pink Floyd

1 oz. sloe gin
1 oz. vodka
½ cup fresh or canned pineapple
Soda water to top
Pineapple spear for garnish

Blend until smooth. Top with soda water. Garnish with a pineapple spear.

Pink Mink

Strawberry liqueur to moisten rim, plus ¼ oz.
    for drink
Coarse sugar for frosting rim
¾ oz. 42Below vodka
¼ oz. Bacardi rum
Ice cubes
½ strawberry for garnish

Moisten the rim of a cocktail glass with strawberry liqueur and dip in sugar. Combine vodka, Bacardi rum, and strawberry liqueur with ice in a shaker. Strain into frosted cocktail glass. Garnish with the strawberry.

Pink Squirrel

2 oz. lemonade
1 oz. UV vodka
Dash grenadine

Shake with ice and strain into a martini glass.

Prairie Oyster

1 egg yolk
2 oz. tomato juice
1 ¼ oz. vodka
Dash Worcestershire sauce
Ice cubes
Salt and freshly ground black pepper to taste

Drop the unbroken egg yolk in the bottom of a chilled wine glass. In a separate mixing glass, combine tomato juice, vodka, and Worcestershire sauce with ice and mix well. Pour over egg yolk, and add salt and pepper.

Purple Passion

2 oz. grape juice
2 oz. grapefruit juice
1 ¼ oz. Sobieski vodka
Ice cubes
Superfine sugar to taste

Combine first three ingredients in a shaker with ice and add superfine sugar. Serve in a Collins glass.

Red

3 oz. cranberry juice
2 oz. Smirnoff green apple vodka
Ice cubes

Pour first two ingredients into a glass over ice and stir well.

Red Panties

1 ½ oz. peach vodka
1 oz. cranberry juice
1 oz. orange juice
½ oz. peach schnapps
Dash grenadine

Shake and strain into a chilled glass.

Rose of Warsaw

1 ½ oz. Sobieski vodka
1 oz. Marie Brizard Cherry liqueur
½ oz. Cointreau
Dash bitters

Shake with ice and strain.

Salty Dog

1 oz. grapefruit juice
1 oz. Smirnoff Red Label vodka
Ice cubes
Course salt for rim

Stir first two ingredients in a shaker and serve over ice in a salt-rimmed glass.

Screwdriver

2 oz. Smirnoff vodka
Orange juice
Ice cubes

Combine first two ingredients and serve in a tall glass with ice.

Seabreeze

2 oz. Sobieski vodka
Ice cubes
Grapefruit juice
Cranberry juice

Pour vodka over ice into a tall glass. Fill halfway with grapefruit juice and top off with cranberry juice.

Silver Bullet

2 oz. Belvedere vodka
¼ oz. Martini & Rossi dry vermouth
Ice cubes
¼ oz. Cutty Sark

Stir the vodka and vermouth on the rocks. Float Cutty Sark on top.

Slim Jim

1 ¼ oz. Sobieski vodka
Diet soda to fill
Lemon or lime slice for garnish

Pour the vodka in a highball glass with ice and add diet soda. Garnish with the lemon or lime slice.

S.O.B.

2 oz. Sobieski vodka
¼ oz. Marie Brizard Blackberry brandy

Pour vodka over blackberry brandy.

Spotted Dog

¾ oz. amaretto
¼ oz. 360 vodka
¼ oz. white crème de cacao
½ cup vanilla ice cream

Mix all ingredients in a blender until smooth.
Pour into a cocktail glass and serve.

Straight Jacket

3 parts Sobieski vodka
1 part Absente liqueur

Shake with ice and serve as a shot, or pour over
ice in a rocks glass.

Sunstroke

3 oz. Tropicana grapefruit juice
1 ¼ oz. vodka
Ice cubes
Dash triple sec

Combine the Tropicana grapefruit juice and vodka on the rocks. Add the triple sec.

Swedish Cocktail

¾ oz. Absolut vodka
¼ oz. gin
¼ oz. white crème de cacao

Combine in a shaker with ice. Strain into a chilled cocktail glass.

Transfusion

2 oz. Sobieski vodka
Ice cubes
Grape juice
Club soda to top

Pour vodka into a tall glass with ice and fill with grape juice. Top with club soda.

Truffle Martini

2 ½ oz. Sobieski vodka
Splash Urbani Tartufi White Truffle Oil

Shake or stir and serve in a chilled martini glass.

The Twist

¾ oz. Smirnoff vodka
½ oz. white crème de menthe
½ oz. orange sherbet

Blend. Pour into a champagne glass.

Vodka and Tonic

2 oz. Sobieski vodka
Tonic
Lime squeeze

Pour vodka into a tall glass over ice and fill with
tonic. Add a squeeze of lime.

Vodka Athens

1 part Absolut vodka
2 dashes lime juice
Dash Angostura bitters
Ginger ale
Ice cubes
Lime wedge for garnish

Build over ice in a highball glass. Garnish with a
wedge of lime.

Vodka Gimlet

2 parts vodka
1 part lime juice
Lemon twist for garnish

Fill shaker with ice. Add vodka and lime juice.
Shake well and pour into a rocks glass. Garnish
with a lemon twist.

Vodka San Francisco

2 oz. Absolut vodka
1 oz. banana liqueur
1 oz. fresh orange juice
Orange wedge for garnish

Shake all ingredients with ice and strain into a
highball glass. Garnish with a wedge of orange.

White Elephant

1 ½ oz. vodka
1 oz. milk
½ oz. white crème de cacao
Ice cubes

Combine in a cocktail shaker. Serve in a tall glass with ice.

White Russian

1 ½ oz. vodka
½ oz. heavy cream
½ oz. Kahlúa
Ice cubes

Shake first three ingredients and serve over ice.

White Spider

2 oz. Sobieski vodka
½ oz. Marie Brizard white crème de menthe
Ice cubes

Stir first two ingredients on the rocks.

Woo Woo

3 ½ oz. cranberry juice
1 ½ oz. vodka
½ oz. peach schnapps
Ice cubes

Serve in a tall glass with ice.

Citrus Vodka

Absolut Squeeze

3 oz. pineapple juice
2 oz. orange juice
1 ¼ oz. Absolut Citron vodka
Splash Chambord for float
Lemon wedge or whole strawberry for garnish

Pour over ice in a tall glass. Top with Chambord and garnish with a lemon wedge or whole strawberry.

B.C.

1 ½ oz. Belvedere Citrus vodka
1 ½ oz. cranberry juice
Ice cubes

Stir on the rocks.

Beach Ball Cooler

1 ¼ oz. Sobieski Cytron vodka
½ oz. crème de cassis
1 tsp. lime juice
Ice cubes
Ginger ale to fill
Lemon slice for garnish
Maraschino cherry for garnish

Mix first three ingredients in a Collins glass with ice. Top with ginger ale and garnish with a lemon slice and a cherry.

Blue Lemonade

1 ¼ oz. Absolut Citron vodka
Splash blue curaçao

Pour over ice in a tall glass.

Cilver Citron

1 ¼ oz. Absolut Citron vodka
½ oz. Mumm champagne Brut Cordon Rouge

Serve straight up.

Citron Breeze

2 oz. cranberry juice
2 oz. grapefruit juice
1 ¼ oz. SKYY Citrus vodka
Ice cubes
Lime slice for garnish

Mix first three ingredients in a chilled Collins glass with ice cubes. Garnish with the lime slice.

Citron Collins

1 ¼ oz. Sobieski Cytron vodka
1 oz. lemon juice
½ oz. sugar syrup
Ice cubes
Maraschino cherry for garnish
Orange slice for garnish

Mix first three ingredients in a Collins glass. Stir well, add ice, and top with club soda. Garnish with the cherry and orange slice.

Citron Godmother

1 ¼ oz. Grey Goose Le Citron vodka
¾ oz. Amaretto di Saronno
Ice cubes

Serve on the rocks.

Citron Kamikaze

¾ oz. Absolut Citron vodka
¾ oz. Cointreau
¾ oz. lime juice
Ice cubes
Lime wedge for garnish

Pour the Absolut Citron, Cointreau, and lime juice over ice in a glass. Shake well and strain into a cocktail glass. Serve straight up or on the rocks. Garnish with the lime.

Citron Madras

1 ¼ oz. Grey Goose Le Citron vodka
Ice cubes
Cranberry juice to fill
Orange juice to fill

Pour vodka in a tall glass with ice, and add equal parts of the two juices.

Citron Martini

1 ¼ oz. Smirnoff Citrus vodka
Dash extra dry vermouth
Lemon twist or olive for garnish

Pour the Smirnoff Citrus vodka and vermouth over ice. Shake or stir well. Strain and serve in a cocktail glass straight up or on the rocks. Garnish with lemon twist or olive.

Citron Rickey

1 ¼ oz. Smirnoff Citrus vodka
Club soda to fill
Squeeze of ¼ fresh lime
Lime wedge for garnish

Pour the vodka in a tall glass with ice and add club soda. Add squeeze of fresh lime and garnish with a lime wedge.

Citron Sour

1 ¼ oz. Sobieski Cytron vodka
¼ oz. lemon juice
1 tsp. sugar syrup
Maraschino cherry for garnish

Mix with ice in a shaker. Strain into a chilled glass.

Lemondrop

1 ¼ oz. Ketel One Citron vodka
Lemon wedge
Superfine sugar

Serve with a wedge of lemon, coated with sugar, on the side. Shoot the vodka, then suck the lemon.

Par 19

1 ½ oz. SKYY Citrus vodka
2 oz. ginger ale
2 oz. grape juice

Pour vodka in a tall glass with ice and fill with ginger ale and grape juice.

Pink Baby

1 ¼ oz. Grey Goose Le Citron vodka
½ oz. Chambord
½ oz. lemon juice
Cracked ice

Mix with cracked ice in a shaker or blender and strain into a chilled cocktail glass.

Pink Lemonade

1 ¼ oz. Smirnoff Citrus vodka
Splash grenadine

Pour over ice in a tall glass.

Rainbow

1 ¼ oz. 3 Olives Citrus vodka
Ice cubes
Grapefruit juice to fill
Grape juice to fill

Pour the 3 Olives Citrus vodka in a tall glass with ice, and fill with equal parts grapefruit juice and grape juice.

Tropical Orchard

4 oz. Tropicana orange juice
1 ¼ oz. Absolut Citron vodka
½ oz. grapefruit juice
½ oz. lime juice
½ oz. triple sec

Mix with cracked ice in a shaker and pour into a chilled double old-fashioned glass.

Twisted Bull

4 oz. beef broth (bouillon)
1 oz. Smirnoff Citrus vodka
Ice cubes
Lime wedge for garnish

Serve over rocks and garnish with the lime wedge.

Twisted Teardrop

1 ½ oz. Smirnoff Citrus vodka
½ oz. triple sec
Cracked ice
Lemon slice for garnish

Mix the first two ingredients with cracked ice in a shaker or blender and pour into a chilled highball glass. Garnish with the lemon slice.

White Citron

2 oz. half-and-half
1 ½ oz. Absolut Citron vodka
½ oz. Kahlúa
Ice cubes

Shake and pour over ice.

Absolut Peppar Vodka

Absohot

½ shot Absolut Peppar vodka
Dash hot sauce
1 bottle Budweiser beer

Mix the Absolut Peppar and hot sauce to taste.
Serve with a Budweiser chaser.

Absolut Peppar Bull Shot

5 oz. beef consommé
1 ¼ oz. Absolut Peppar vodka
1 tsp. lemon juice
5 dashes Worcestershire sauce
Pinch celery salt or seed
Ice cubes

Mix ingredients in a 14-oz. double old-fashioned
glass.

Absolut Salt and Peppar

1 ¼ oz. Absolut Peppar vodka
Course salt for rim
Cucumber spear for garnish

Pour chilled vodka into a salt-rimmed cocktail glass. Garnish with the cucumber spear.

Black Peppar

1 ¼ oz. Absolut Peppar vodka
¼ oz. blackberry brandy
Ice cubes

Shake and strain into a shot glass.

Cajun Mary

4 oz. tomato juice
1 ¼ oz. Absolut Peppar
Juice ½ lemon
½ tsp. horseradish
2 dashes Worcestershire sauce
Dash celery salt
Dash salt
Ice cubes
Celery stalk for garnish

Combine first seven ingredients. Fill an 8-oz. glass with ice and pour in mixture. Garnish with the celery stalk.

Doyle's Mulligan

1 oz. Absolut Peppar vodka
4 oz. Budweiser beer

Add the Absolut Peppar slowly into the beer.

Dragon Fire

1 oz. Absolut Peppar vodka
¼ oz. green crème de menthe

Serve on the rocks.

Firebird

4 oz. cranberry juice
1 ¼ oz. Absolut Peppar vodka
Ice cubes

Serve on the rocks.

The Flame

1 ¼ oz. Absolut Peppar
¼ oz. Chambord
Ice cubes

Serve on the rocks.

Hot Pants

1 oz. peach schnapps
¼ oz. Absolut Peppar vodka
Ice cubes

Serve on the rocks.

Long Island Hot Tea

¼ oz. Absolut Peppar vodka
¼ oz. Bacardi rum
¼ oz. Bombay gin
¼ oz. sweet-and-sour mix
¼ oz. tequila
Ice cubes
Cola to fill

Mix first five ingredients and serve in a tall glass filled with ice. Top with cola.

Scorpion's Sting

1 ¼ oz. Absolut Peppar vodka
¼ oz. white crème de menthe
Ice cubes

Serve in a rocks glass over ice.

Sparks

3 oz. chilled Mumm champagne
1 oz. chilled Absolut Peppar

Serve in a champagne glass.

Swedish Bull

4 oz. beef broth (bouillon)
1 ¼ oz. Absolut Peppar vodka
Ice cubes
Lime wedge for garnish

Serve on the rocks and garnish with a lime wedge.

Tear Drop

1 ¼ oz. Absolut Peppar vodka
¼ oz. triple sec
Ice cubes
Maraschino cherry for garnish

Shake the first two ingredients with ice and strain into a shot glass. Garnish with the cherry.

Volcano

1 ¼ oz. Absolut Peppar
Dash grenadine
Ice cubes

Mix and strain into a shot glass.

Algonquin

Ice cubes
2 oz. bourbon
1 oz. dry vermouth
1 oz. fresh pineapple juice
1 maraschino cherry for garnish

Fill a cocktail shaker halfway with ice cubes. Pour in the bourbon, vermouth, and pineapple juice. Using a bar spoon or iced tea spoon, gently stir until the drink is very cold. Pour the entire mixture into an old-fashioned glass, or strain the mixture into a cocktail glass. Garnish with the cherry.

Angelic

2 oz. half-and-half
1 oz. Wild Turkey bourbon
½ oz. white crème de cacao
Dash grenadine
Ice cubes

Shake. Serve on the rocks or strain into cocktail glass.

Beehive

2 oz. grapefruit juice
2 oz. Wild Turkey Honey bourbon
Ice cubes

Shake well and serve on the rocks.

Bionic Turkey

1 oz. orange juice
1 oz. Wild Turkey bourbon
½ oz. sweet vermouth
Dash yellow chartreuse
Ice cubes

Shake and serve on the rocks.

Bourbon Collins

4-5 oz. sweetened lemon mix
1 ½ oz. Wild Turkey bourbon
Ice cubes
Club soda to fill

Shake first two ingredients with ice and pour into tall glass with ice. Fill with club soda.

Bourbon Delight

1 oz. Wild Turkey bourbon
½ oz. lemon juice
¼ oz. crème de menthe
¼ oz. sweet vermouth
Ice cubes

Shake and serve on the rocks.

Bourbon Manhattan

1 ¼ oz. bourbon
¼ oz. sweet vermouth
3 dashes Angostura bitters
Maraschino cherry

Stir first three ingredients on the rocks or strain into cocktail glass. Add cherry.

Bourbon Old-Fashioned

1 maraschino cherry
1 orange slice
1 ½ oz. bourbon
¼ tsp. sugar
2 dashes Angostura bitters

Muddle cherry and orange slice in bottom of old-fashioned glass. Add remaining ingredients and stir well.

Brass Knuckle

2 oz. sweetened lemon mix
1 ½ oz. bourbon
½ oz. triple sec
Ice cubes

Shake and serve on the rocks.

The Canadian Dry Manhattan

2 oz. Canadian Club
½ oz. Martini & Rossi dry vermouth
Olive and/or lemon twist (optional)

Pour ingredients into an ice-filled mixing glass and stir. Strain into a prechilled cocktail glass.

The Canadian-Perfect Manhattan

2 oz. Canadian Club
¼ oz. Martini & Rossi extra dry vermouth
¼ oz. Martini & Rossi Rosso sweet vermouth
Maraschino cherry, olive, or lemon twist for
    garnish (optional)

Pour ingredients into an ice-filled mixing glass
and stir. Strain into a prechilled cocktail glass
and add garnish, if desired.

The Canadian Sweet Manhattan

2 oz. Canadian Club
½ oz. Martini & Rossi Rosso sweet vermouth
Maraschino cherry or lemon twist for garnish
    (optional)

Pour ingredients into an ice-filled mixing glass
and stir. Strain into a prechilled cocktail glass
and garnish, if desired.

Chapel Hill

Ice cubes
1 ½ oz. bourbon
½ oz. freshly squeezed lemon juice
½ oz. triple sec
Orange twist for garnish

Fill a cocktail shaker halfway with ice cubes. Pour the remaining ingredients into the shaker and shake until the drink is cold. Strain into a cocktail glass. Garnish with the orange twist.

Colonel Hayden

3 oz. pineapple juice
1 ½ oz. Old Grand Dad bourbon
¾ oz. apricot brandy
Ice cubes

Shake and serve on the rocks.

Commodore

1 oz. crème de cacao
1 oz. Old Grand Dad bourbon
1 oz. sweetened lemon juice
Dash grenadine
Ice cubes

Shake and serve on the rocks.

Dixie

2 oz. bourbon
¼ oz. triple sec
¼ oz. white crème de menthe
Dash Angostura bitters
Ice cubes
Lemon twist for garnish

Shake first five ingredients and serve on the rocks with a lemon twist.

Dizzy Lizzy

1 ½ oz. bourbon
1 ½ oz. sherry
Dash lemon juice
Ice cubes
Club soda to fill

Pour the first three ingredients into a tall glass with ice, and fill with club soda.

Gobbler

1 ½ oz. Wild Turkey bourbon
Dash grenadine
Ice cubes
Orange juice to fill

Put the first two ingredients into a tall glass with ice, and fill with orange juice.

Grandfather

2 oz. bourbon
1 oz. Amaretto di Saronno
Ice cubes

Stir on the rocks.

Grand Fellow

1 part Old Grand Dad bourbon
1 part sweet vermouth
Dash Angostura bitters

Stir on the rocks or strain into cocktail glass.

Hot Apple Cobbler

1 ½ oz. Wild Turkey bourbon
Hot apple cider
Cinnamon stick for garnish

Fill with hot apple cider. Garnish with a cinnamon stick.

Kentucky Cocktail

2 oz. pineapple juice
1 ½ oz. bourbon
Ice cubes

Shake and serve on the rocks or strain into a cocktail glass.

Lynchburg Lemonade

Ice cubes
1 ½ oz. Jack Daniel's
1 oz. sour mix
1 oz. triple sec
Lemon-lime soda as needed

Fill a highball glass with ice cubes. Add all ingredients but lemon-lime soda. Stir to combine. Top off the glass with the lemon-lime soda.

Minty Julep

1 oz. bourbon
½ oz. green crème de menthe
Ice cubes

Add splash of water and stir on the rocks.

Perfect Turkey Manhattan

4 parts Wild Turkey bourbon
1 part extra dry vermouth
1 part sweet vermouth
Ice cubes
Lemon twist for garnish

Stir first three ingredients on the rocks or strain
into cocktail glass. Add lemon twist.

Presbyterian

2 oz. ginger ale
2 oz. soda water
1 ¼ oz. bourbon
Lemon twist

Stir together in a highball glass with ice cubes.
Twist lemon peel over drink and drop in.

Sloe Bird

1 oz. Wild Turkey bourbon
½ oz. lemon juice
½ oz. sloe gin
1 tsp. superfine sugar
Ice cubes

Stir in mixing glass. Strain into a cocktail glass.

Sour Turkey

1 ½ oz. lemon juice
1 ½ oz. Wild Turkey bourbon
½ tsp. superfine sugar
Lemon slice for garnish
Maraschino cherry for garnish

In a cocktail shaker with ice, mix well. Strain into a chilled sour glass and garnish with a lemon slice and a cherry.

Southern Love

Ice cubes
1 oz. amaretto
1 oz. bourbon
6 oz. cola

Fill an oversized cocktail or old-fashioned glass with ice cubes. Let sit for 2 to 3 minutes to chill glass. Holding the ice so it doesn't fall out, discard any melted water. Pour in the amaretto and bourbon, and top with cola. Stir and serve.

Steve's Sour

2 ½ oz. Old Grand Dad Bourbon
1 ½ oz. orange juice
1 ½ oz. sweetened lemon mix

Street Car

Ice cubes
2 oz. bourbon
½ oz. crème de cassis
Splash vanilla simple syrup
Juice 1 lime
1 tbsp. blueberry compote
Fresh blueberries for garnish

Fill a cocktail shaker halfway with ice cubes. Combine ingredients in shake and shake vigorously until the drink is well chilled. Strain into a cocktail glass. Garnish with a few blueberries.

Turkey and Cola

Ice cubes
1 ½ oz. Wild Turkey bourbon
Cola to fill

Fill a tall glass with ice, add bourbon, and fill with cola.

Turkey Shoot

1 ¼ oz. Wild Turkey bourbon
Anisette

Add bourbon to a pony glass, and float anisette on top. Serve as a shot.

Washington Apple

Ice cubes
1 ½ oz. bourbon
1 ½ oz. DeKuyper Apple Pucker schnapps
1 ½ oz. cranberry juice
1 apple slice or wedge for garnish

Fill a cocktail shaker halfway with ice cubes.
Pour ingredients into the shaker. Shake vigorously until the drink is cold. Strain into a cocktail
glass. Garnish with the apple.

Wild Mint Julep

2 tsp. water
1 tsp. sugar
2–3 mint sprigs
Crushed ice
1 ½ oz. Wild Turkey bourbon

In a tall glass, muddle water, sugar, and mint. Fill
with crushed ice and add Wild Turkey. Stir until
well frosted.

Wild Sour

1 ½ oz. orange juice
1 ½ oz. sweetened lemon mix
1 ½ oz. Wild Turkey bourbon

Shake with ice and serve on the rocks.

W.T. Fizz

Ice cubes
2 oz. Wild Turkey bourbon
Club soda to fill
Squeeze of lemon, lime, or orange
Slice of lemon, lime, or orange for garnish

Fill a highball glass with ice, add bourbon, and fill with club soda. Add a squeeze of fresh lemon, lime, or orange. Garnish with a slice of the same fruit.

Canadian Club Cocktail Glass Time

We present here the most noted of the whiskey cocktails, employing the best whiskey to make them with, Canadian Club. *À votre santé.*

Black Hawk

2 oz. Canadian Club
1 oz. sloe gin
Maraschino cherry for garnish

Pour ingredients into an ice-filled mixing glass and stir. Pour into a prechilled cocktail glass and garnish with a cherry.

Bounty

2 oz. Canadian Club
¼ oz. Benedictine
¼ oz. Martini & Rossi Rosso sweet vermouth
Lemon or orange twist for garnish (optional)

Pour ingredients into an ice-filled mixing glass and stir vigorously. Strain into a prechilled cocktail glass and garnish, if desired.

Canadian Club Cocktail

2 oz. Canadian Club
1 tsp. sugar syrup
Dash Angostura bitters
Maraschino cherry for garnish

Pour ingredients into an ice-filled mixing glass. Strain into a prechilled cocktail glass and garnish with the cherry.

Fox River

2 oz. Canadian Club
1 tbsp. dark crème de cacao
4 dashes Angostura bitters

Pour ingredients into an ice-filled mixing glass and stir. Strain into a cocktail glass.

Frisco

1 ½ oz. Canadian Club
¾ oz. Benedictine
Lemon twist for garnish

Stir ingredients with cracked ice. Strain into a cocktail glass and garnish with a lemon twist.

Irish Canadian

1 ½ oz. Canadian Club
½ oz. Irish Mist

Stir ingredients with ice until well mixed. Strain into a cocktail glass.

Lawhill

1 ½ oz. Canadian Club
¾ oz. Martini & Rossi extra dry vermouth
¼ tsp. anisette
¼ tsp. maraschino liqueur
Dash Angostura bitters

Pour ingredients into an ice-filled mixing glass. Strain into a cocktail glass.

Maple Leaf

1 oz. Canadian Club
1 oz. heavy cream
½ oz. Irish Mist
1 tsp. crème de cacao

Shake all ingredients vigorously with ice and strain into a cocktail glass.

Monte Carlo

¾ oz. Canadian Club
¾ oz. Dubonnet
Dash Angostura bitters
Lemon twist for garnish

Pour ingredients into an ice-filled mixing glass
and stir vigorously. Strain into a prechilled cocktail glass.

Canadian Club Old-Fashioned Enjoyments

The classic Old-Fashioned is truly a magnificent cocktail and is but one drink served in what is called an old-fashioned glass. Herewith, we present a batch to be served in the aforementioned glassware, and to be enjoyed for their old-fashioned flavor, their old-fashioned elegance—their old-fashioned ambiance. Point being, there is nothing old-fashioned about an old-fashioned—especially if it's made with the premier whisky—Canadian Club. Here's looking at you.

Canadian Stone Sour

1 ¼ oz. Canadian Club
1 oz. orange juice
1 oz. sweet-and-sour mix
Maraschino cherry for garnish
Orange slice for garnish

Pour the ingredients into a cocktail shaker with ice. Shake and strain into sour glass and garnish with the cherry and orange slice.

Commodore Cocktail

1 ¼ oz. Canadian Club
1 oz. sweet-and-sour mix
2 dashes Angostura bitters
Dash lime juice (optional)

Pour ingredients into a cocktail shaker with ice
and shake. Strain into a prechilled glass.

Palmer Cocktail

1 ¼ oz. Canadian Club
1 oz. lemon juice
2 dashes Angostura bitters

Pour ingredients into a mixing glass filled with
ice cubes. Stir and strain into a prechilled glass.

Quebec

2 oz. Canadian Club
¼ oz. Campari or Amer Picon bitters
¼ oz. maraschino cherry juice
¼ oz. sweet vermouth
Ice cubes
Maraschino cherry for garnish

Pour first four ingredients into a cocktail shaker
with ice. Shake and pour over ice cubes in a
double old-fashioned or rocks glass. Garnish with
the cherry.

Ward Eight Collins

2 oz. sweet-and-sour mix
1 ¼ oz. Canadian Club
¼ oz. grenadine
Ice cubes
Club soda to fill
Lime squeeze for garnish

Pour first four ingredients into a cocktail shaker with ice. Shake and strain into a Collins glass filled with ice cubes and add soda. Insert long straws.

Windsor Collins

2 oz. sweet-and-sour mix
1 oz. Canadian Club
½ oz. peach schnapps
½ oz. triple sec
Ice cubes
Lime squeeze for garnish

Pour the first four ingredients into a cocktail shaker with ice. Shake and strain into a Collins glass with ice cubes. Add a squeeze of lime for garnish.

Yukon Cocktail

1 ½ oz. Canadian Club
¼ oz. triple sec
2 dashes Angostura bitters
1 tsp. superfine sugar

Pour ingredients into a cocktail shaker with ice and shake. Strain into a prechilled glass.

WINE AND CHAMPAGNE

American Flyer

1 ½ oz. light rum
1 tbsp. lime juice
½ tsp. simple sugar syrup
2 oz. champagne or sparkling wine

Shake first three ingredients together. Strain into a chilled wine goblet. Top with champagne.

American Rose

¼ oz. brandy
¼ oz. peach schnapps
¼ oz. Pernod
Splash grenadine
2 oz. Korbel extra dry champagne

Add to champagne glass. Stir gently.

Arise My Love

3 oz. champagne
¼ oz. green crème de menthe

Stir gently.

Bacardi Champagne Cocktail

1 oz. Bacardi Silver Rum
1 tsp. sugar
Dash bitters
3 oz. champagne

In a tall glass mix rum, sugar, and bitters. Fill with champagne.

Bellini

1 peach half
¼ oz. simple syrup
2 oz. champagne

Muddle peach in a champagne glass with simple syrup. Fill the glass with champagne.

Bishop Cocktail

2 oz. red wine
1 oz. rum
⅛ oz. lime juice
⅛ oz. simple syrup

Bloody Rum Punch

1 oz. red wine
1 oz. rum
½ oz. lime juice
½ oz. simple syrup (hot water and sugar)
½ oz. triple sec

Stir. Pour into a 6-oz. wine glass.

Blue Bubbles

3 oz. Korbel extra dry champagne
¼ oz. blueberry schnapps
Splash blue curaçao

Pour into champagne glass and stir gently.

Blue Velvet

3 oz. champagne
Splash blue curaçao

Serve in a flute.

California Sunshine

3 oz. champagne
1 oz. orange juice
¼ oz. crème de cassis

Cardinal Cocktail

3 oz. red wine
1 oz. crème de cassis

Champagne Cocktail

3 oz. chilled champagne
1 cube sugar
Dash Angostura bitters
Lemon twist for garnish

Stir first three ingredients slowly. Garnish with a lemon twist.

Champagne Cocktail No. 2

4 oz. chilled Korbel extra dry champagne
1 oz. Southern Comfort bourbon
Dash Angostura bitters
Lemon twist for garnish

Pour first three ingredients into fluted champagne glass. Garnish with lemon twist.

Champagne Cocktail No. 3

1 oz. brandy
4 oz. chilled champagne
Orange twist for garnish

Pour brandy into champagne glass, fill with champagne, and garnish with the orange twist.

Champagne Fizz

Ice cubes
1 ½ oz. gin
1 oz. lemon juice
1 tsp. superfine sugar
3 oz. chilled champagne

In a shaker half-filled with ice cubes, combine the gin, lemon juice, and sugar. Shake well. Strain into a champagne flute. Add the champagne.

Champagne Normandy

3 oz. chilled champagne
1 oz. Calvados
1 tsp. sugar
Dash Angostura bitters
Orange slice for garnish

Serve in a champagne glass; add an orange slice.

Dawn

3 oz. champagne
1 oz. Fino sherry
Splash fresh lime juice

Stir and serve in a cocktail glass.

Death in the Afternoon

1 ½ oz. Pernod
3 oz. champagne

Pour Pernod into a chilled champagne glass. Fill the glass with champagne.

French Kiss

3 oz. champagne
1 oz. vodka
1 tbsp. Lillet Blanc
Orange twist for garnish

 OLIVER'S, SEATTLE, WA

Kir or Kir Royale

3 oz. champagne
Splash crème de cassis

Fill the glass with champagne and add a splash of crème de cassis.

Liquid Lust

2 oz. white wine
½ oz. club soda
½ oz. cranberry juice
½ oz. orange juice
½ oz. tequila
Maraschino cherry for garnish
Orange slice for garnish

Midori Cocktail

3 oz. champagne
1 oz. Midori Melon liqueur

Serve in fluted champagne glass.

Mimosa

3 oz. champagne
2 oz. orange juice

Combine in a champagne flute and stir.

Nelson's Blood

3 oz. champagne
½ oz. tawny port

Stir slowly but well.

Passion Mimosa

3 oz. champagne
1 oz. Alizé liqueur
Strawberry for garnish

Pink California Sunshine

4 oz. chilled orange juice
4 oz. pink champagne
Dash crème de cassis

Poinsetta

4 oz. champagne
1 oz. cranberry juice
Orange slice for garnish

Raspberry Truffle

4 oz. champagne
1 oz. Stolichnya Razberi vodka
1 splash Godiva chocolate liqueur

Serve in a flute.

Rose Berry Bliss

2 oz. Clos du Bois Rosé
2 oz. lemon-lime soda
1 oz. pink lemonade
4 blueberries

Serve in large wine glass.

Ruby Red

4 oz. champagne
1 oz. Stoli Razberi Vodka
Splash crème de cassis

Serve in a flute.

 THE BUBBLE LOUNGE, NEW YORK, NY

Sangría

2 oz. red wine
¼ oz. brandy
¼ oz. club soda
¼ oz. curaçao
¼ oz. fresh lemon or lime juice
¼ oz. fresh orange juice
¼ oz. ginger ale
¼ oz. sugar syrup

Serve in large wine glass. Stir over rocks or straight up.

Scotch Fizz

3 oz. pink champagne
1 oz. scotch

Scotch Royale

1 tsp. superfine sugar
1 ½ oz. scotch
Dash Angostura bitters
3 oz. champagne to fill

Dissolve sugar in scotch and bitters in a champagne flute. Fill with champagne. Stir gently.

Something Blue

2 oz. white wine
½ oz. ginger ale
½ oz. Hpnotiq liqueur
Ice cubes

Serve over ice in a wine glass.

Sputnik

3 oz. champagne
1 oz. fresh orange juice
1 oz. Stolichnaya Ohranj vodka
Splash grenadine syrup

Thug Passion

3 oz. champagne
2 oz. Alizé

Velvet Swing

3 oz. champagne
2 oz. ruby port
Splash Armagnac

Serve in a flute.

Witches' Brew

3 oz. champagne
1 oz. Strega liqueur

Pour into chilled champagne glass.

YOUR COCKTAIL RECIPES

DRINK INDEX

ALCOHOL INDEX

ABOUT THE AUTHOR

Ray Foley, a former marine with more than thirty years of bartending and restaurant experience, is the founder and editor of *Bartender Magazine*. Ray is referred to as "The Legend" for all he has done for bartenders and bartending. *Bartender Magazine* is the only magazine in the world specifically geared toward bartenders and is one of the very few primarily designed for servers of alcohol. *Bartender Magazine* is enjoying its thirty-second year and currently has a steadily growing circulation of more than one hundred thousand.

After serving in the United States Marine Corps and attending Seton Hall University, Ray entered the restaurant business as a bartender, which eventually led to a job as the assistant general manager of The Manor in West Orange, New Jersey, with more than 350 employees.

In 1983, Ray left The Manor to devote his full efforts to *Bartender Magazine*. The circulation and exposure has grown from seven thousand to more than one hundred thousand to date and has become the largest on-premise liquor magazine in the country.

Ray has been published in numerous articles throughout the country and has appeared on many TV and radio shows. He is the founder of the Bartender Hall of Fame, which honors the best bartenders throughout the United States, not only for their abilities at bartending but also for their involvement and service in their communities.

Ray is also the founder of The Bartenders' Foundation Incorporated. This nonprofit foundation has been set up to raise scholarship money for bartenders and their families. Scholarships awarded to bartenders can be used to either further their education or can go toward the education of their children.

Ray is the founder of www.bartender.com, www.mixologist.com, www.USBartender.com, and many other bar-related websites.

Mr. Foley serves as a consultant to some of our nation's foremost distillers and importers. He is also responsible for creating and naming new drinks for the liquor industry. Here are just a few:

"The Fuzzy Navel"

"The Royal Stretch"—for Grand Royal Oaks Race

"The Royal Turf"—for Grand Royal Oaks Race

"Pink Cadillac"

"Pear-A-Terre"

"Grapeful Red"

"Pear A Mud"

"Pearsian Kat"

"Pomtree Cocktail"
"The Royal Sour"
"The Hamptons"
"Golden Apfel"
"Mosquito Bite"

Ray has one of the largest collections of cocktail recipe books in the world, dating back to the 1800s, and is one of the foremost collectors of cocktail shakers, having 368 shakers in his collection.

He is the author of the following bestsellers:

Bartending for Dummies
Running a Bar for Dummies
The Ultimate Little Frozen Drinks Book
The Ultimate Little Shooter Book
The Ultimate Little Martini Book
Advice from Anonymous
The Best Irish Drinks
Jokes, Quotes, and Bartoons
Beer is the Answer... What is the Question?
X-Rated Drinks
Bartender Magazine's Ultimate Bartender's Guide
Vodka 1000
Rum 1000
Tequila 1000
The Best Summer Drinks
God Loves Golfers Best

Ray resides in New Jersey with his wife and partner of twenty-nine years, Jackie, and their son, Ryan.